Saddam's War

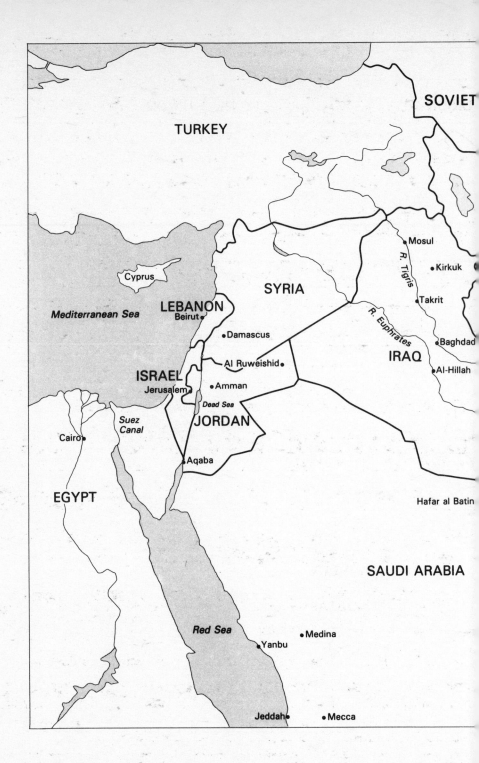

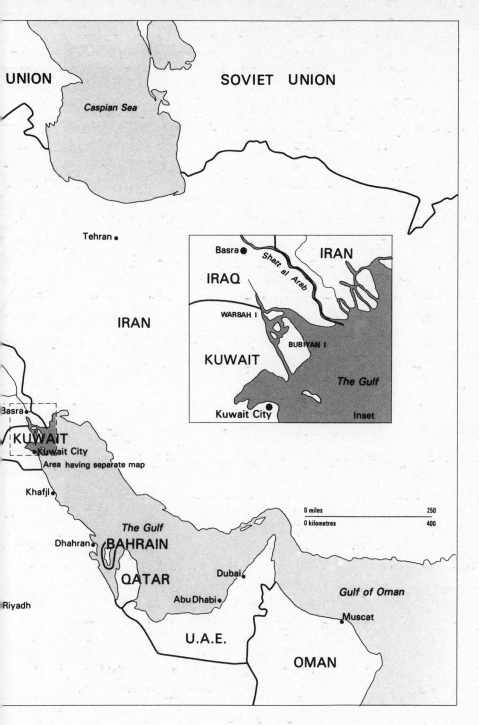

By the same authors

THE GULF WAR

SADDAM'S WAR

*The Origins of the Kuwait Conflict
and the International Response*

John Bulloch
and Harvey Morris

faber and faber

LONDON · BOSTON

First published in 1991
by Faber and Faber Limited
3 Queen Square London WC1N 3AU
Reprinted 1991

Photoset by Parker Typesetting Service Leicester
Printed in England by Clays Ltd St Ives plc

A CIP record for this book
is available from the British Library
ISBN 0 571 16387 4

Contents

Illustrations

Acknowledgements

Our thanks are due to many people who have helped us in the very rapid preparation of this book, with information, insight or analysis. During our researches, we visited Baghdad, Jeddah, Taif, Sanaa, Muscat, Abu Dhabi, Amman, Jerusalem, Athens, and Paris, while doing most of our work in London. In each centre we were given invaluable help by local officials and diplomats. In Baghdad the help of the British and United States embassies was invaluable, while the Iraqi director of information, Naji al-Hadithi, applied the lessons he had learnt while press counsellor in London to translate Iraqi views into understandable Western concepts – and in the process, renewed old friendships. In Amman a similar role was played by the minister of information and former ambassador in London, Ibrahim Izzedin, while in Jerusalem, such distinguished dissendents as Radwan Ayesh made sense out of apparent turmoil.

We are indebted to Adel Darwish for technical help as well as his knowledge of Egyptian affairs, to John Parker for coming to the rescue in an emergency, and to many other colleagues. Our thanks are also due to the foreign editors of the *Independent* and the *Independent on Sunday*, who allowed us to concentrate so firmly on events in the Gulf. We are particularly grateful to Sir Anthony Parsons, the distinguished former ambassador, and to Efraim Karsh of Kings College, London, for reading the typescript and for their penetrating and helpful comments, but we emphasize that the interpretations and the judgements, and above all the mistakes, are entirely our own.

London and Oxfordshire
December 1990

Preface

Saddam's War is not intended as a comprehensive history of the Kuwait crisis nor as a biography of its main protagonist. Instead we have tried to examine the origins of Iraq's invasion of Kuwait on 2 August 1990 and to explain the nature of the man and the regime responsible for the first important international crisis of the post-Cold War era.

We have also attempted to undo certain preconceptions about the crisis: that it was only about oil; that the invasion was a purely Arab affair which should have been left to the Arabs to solve; that Saddam's interest in invading his southern neighbour was essentially economic.

There were many who questioned the nature and extent of the US-led response to Saddam's invasion. To put it at its simplest: was Kuwait worth a war? But the crisis was never just about restoring the independence of Kuwait. With his annexation of a sovereign state, Saddam challenged the very basis of international relations within the United Nations, just at a time when that body was emerging from the Cold War era as an effective forum for the resolution of international disputes.

There were those who saw the crisis as principally a US affair, focusing on the United States' desire to establish its domination of the Middle East; and yet a remarkable international consensus backed the American position, reflected in numerous UN resolutions and in the decision of more than twenty countries to participate, alongside US forces, in the international coalition confronting Saddam. Even Iraq's nominal supporters, the PLO, Jordan and Yemen, did not condone the annexation. To a greater or lesser degree all states subscribed to President Bush's declaration that the occupation of Kuwait would not be allowed to stand.

From the dispatch of the first US troops it was clear that the crisis could only end in one of two ways: either in a war or in Iraq's voluntary withdrawal from Kuwait. It is interesting that, from the very first, a majority of our Western contacts saw the crisis ending in war, while most of our Middle Eastern sources predicted that Saddam would eventually withdraw.

We have paid particular attention to Saddam's rise to power within the Baath Party, both to underline the nature of the Iraqi regime and as a reminder that, at the time of the invasion, Saddam had been the effective ruler of one of the Middle East's most powerful states for more than twenty years. We have also dwelt at some length on the consequences of the Gulf war and, more particularly, on the two years between the ceasefire with Iran and the invasion of Kuwait. In that period, Saddam gave many indications of his aggressive intentions, most of which were ignored by the international community. But we do not argue that the United States and others, having supported Iraq in the past and then having overlooked the threat it posed, had somehow lost the right to check his ambitions in 1990.

In the chapters on Saddam Hussein and his rise to power, we have given instances of the brutality of the regime in order to underline its totalitarian nature. But we have tried to avoid presenting a gruesome catalogue of crimes to justify his popular image as the Butcher of Baghdad. It is an image which has been promoted almost as much by the regime as by its opponents; fear is a powerful weapon in Saddam's armoury of internal represssion. For this reason, some sources were willing to speak to us only on condition of anonymity. Wherever sources are not named, this is at their request.

A number of general points concerning international relations in the post-Cold War period emerge from a study of the Kuwait crisis. It highlighted the importance of human rights as a measure of the legitimacy of a regime; criticism of human rights violations can no longer be regarded as interference in the affairs of a sovereign state;

and censure of or sanctions against violators cannot be applied selectively. Western states have cited human rights violations as a means of applying diplomatic pressure on, among others, the Soviet Union and China, but grave violations by Iraq were largely overlooked.

Another factor which has been highlighted is the short-sightedness of arming regimes which oppress their own people and threaten others. Once the crisis is resolved, the least suitable security structure for the Gulf is the one most likely to emerge – an unstable balance of power between the potentially antagonistic regimes of Iraq, Iran and Saudi Arabia, which will continue to receive weapons transfers from the industrialized states.

We have tried to present an analysis of the origins of the Kuwait invasion which acknowledges the failure of both the West and the Arabs to recognize the threat posed by Iraq. Our central contention, however, is that one man, Saddam Hussein, was responsible for all the consequences of the aggression. It is perverse to argue, as some of Iraq's apologists have done, that the crisis was somehow the responsibility of the United States or Kuwait.

The invasion was a deliberate stage in Saddam's war, a war which he waged against his political opponents, against his own people, against Iran and in which, ultimately, he threatened to embroil the rest of the world.

NOTE

No attempt has been made in this book to give a scholarly transliteration of Arabic or Persian names for people or places. The style adopted is the one generally used in British or French newspapers.

Chronology

1958

14 July   Iraq monarchy overthrown in popular coup by 'Free Officers' and the Republic of Iraq established. Brigadier Abdel Karim Qassem becomes prime minister.

24 July   Baath party founder Michel Aflaq arrives in Baghdad.

1959

7 October   Baathist hit-team which includes Saddam Hussein tries to assassinate Qassem. Saddam flees to Syria and then Egypt.

1961

19 June   Kuwait becomes fully independent.

25 June   Iraq publicly renews its claim that Kuwait is part of Iraq.

3 July   British forces arrive in Kuwait to defend the emirate against Iraq.

1963

8 February   Qassem overthrown by Baath coup in 'Ramadan Revolution'. Abdel Salem Aref becomes president. Saddam Hussein returns from exile in Egypt.

18 November   President Aref takes direct control with army backing and dismisses Baathist ministers.

1968

17 July   Baath party seizes power in Iraq. Revolutionary government formed under Ahmed Hassan al-Bakr.

| 30 July | Consolidation of the revolution. Ahmed Hassan al-Bakr becomes chairman of the Revolutionary Command Council, and Saddam Hussein deputy chairman in charge of internal security. |

1972

8 April	Iraq and Soviet Union conclude fifteen-year Treaty of Friendship and Co-operation.
30 May	President Nixon announces that the Shah of Iran can buy any non-nuclear weapons he wants, and promises American co-operation with Iran.
1 June	Iraqi oil nationalization.

1973

| 20 March | Iraq seizes two Kuwaiti border posts, but withdraws as a result of international pressure. |
| 20 August | Sheikh Jaber, prime minister of Kuwait, in Baghdad for border talks. |

1975

| 6 March | Accord signed in Algiers between Iran and Iraq giving Iran control of Shatt al-Arab waterway in return for an end to Iranian support for Kurdish insurgents inside Iraq. |
| 17 September | Algiers Accord ratified by Iran and Iraq. |

1978

| 11 October | Ayatollah Khomeini expelled from Iraq. |

1979

16 July	Saddam Hussein becomes President of Iraq, chairman of the Revolutionary Command Council, and Commander-in-Chief of the armed forces.
30 October	Iraq demands revision of Algiers agreement.
4 November	Militant students seize US embassy in Tehran and take hostages.

1980

| 4 September | Iraq claims war with Iran began. |

17 September   Iraq abrogates Algiers agreement.
22 September   Iraq invades Iran.

1981
20 January   US hostages freed in Tehran.
7 June   Israeli jets bomb Iraq's Osirak nuclear reactor.

1982
6 June   Israel invades Lebanon.
30 June   Iraq announces unilateral withdrawal from Iranian territory.

1984
1 March   First confirmed use of poison gas by Iraq.

1987
20 July   UN Security Council passes Resolution 598 calling for ceasefire between Iran and Iraq.
22 July   US Navy begins escorting Kuwaiti tankers.

1988
29 February   First Iraqi use of long-range missiles to hit Iranian cities.
28 March   Some 5,000 people killed in Iraqi gas attack on Halabja.
18 July   Iran formally accepts Resolution 598 and Gulf war ends.

1989
17 August   Explosion at al-Hillah munitions factory. British-based journalist Farzad Bazoft visits site to investigate.
15 September   Bazoft and British nurse Daphne Parish arrested.

1990
15 March   Farzad Bazoft executed.
28 May   Arab League summit conference in Baghdad.
18 July   Iraqi Foreign Minister Tareq Aziz tells Arab League that Kuwait has stolen $2.4 billion of Iraqi oil.

24 July	President Hosni Mubarak of Egypt visits Iraq, Kuwait and Saudi Arabia in an attempt to mediate as Iraq deploys troops along the Kuwait border.
25 July	US Ambassador in Iraq meets Saddam Hussein.
27 July	OPEC agrees to raise oil reference price to $21 a barrel.
31 July	Iraqi and Kuwait officials meet in Jeddah.
1 August	Jeddah talks collapse.
2 August	Iraq invades Kuwait.

Iraq and the New World Order

At a regular briefing on the afternoon of Monday 30 July 1990 the State Department deputy spokesman, Richard Boucher, revealed that the United States had no plans to intervene in Trinidad. This was despite the fact that law and order had broken down in this corner of America's backyard, and the prime minister, Arthur Robinson, was being held hostage at gunpoint by Muslim militants. 'The Trinidadians would like to find a solution on their own without any outside assistance,' said Boucher. 'They'd just rather settle it themselves.'

It is unlikely that Saddam Hussein picked up this signal of the Bush administration's reluctance to intervene in foreign disputes. He was preoccupied that day. On the eve of what were to be the final talks between Iraq and Kuwait on Baghdad's claims against the emirate he was preparing the invasion of his southern neighbour.

But the Iraqis would not have overlooked another signal from Washington. Three days earlier, the State Department had criticized a Senate vote banning US agricultural loans to Iraq, in response to Iraq's bullying tactics against Kuwait. This time, Mr Boucher acknowledged that Iraq's recent behaviour had 'caused us concern' and that the White House was looking at possible export controls. But he added that the administration felt Congress's actions 'would not help us achieve our goals'.

Only the Republican senator Alfonse D'Amato of New York anticipated the mood that was to prevail throughout the United States and much of the world within just a few days. He denounced Saddam Hussein as 'a butcher, a killer, a bully. Some day we're going to have to stand up to him. Why not now?'

D'Amato's diatribe had an old-fashioned Cold War ring, even though it was directed at a new potential enemy rather than at the traditional foe, the Soviet Union. It was language at odds with the new world order in which co-operation and compromise seemed destined to replace the politics of confrontation.

It was certainly very different from the tone adopted by assistant secretary of state John Kelly when he testified at the House of Representatives Foreign Affairs Committee just two days before the invasion. Asked by the Democrat, Lee Hamilton, what precisely was the US commitment to supporting its friends in the Gulf, Kelly replied: 'We have no defence treaty relationship with any Gulf country. That is clear. We support the security and independence of friendly states in the region . . . We have historically avoided taking a position on border disputes or on internal OPEC deliberations, but we have certainly, as have all administrations, resoundingly called for the peaceful settlement of disputes and differences in the area.' This must have sounded to the Iraqis like a guarantee of non-intervention.

The soft-pedalling on the loans issue was not the first time that the US administration had moved to head off congressional action against Iraq. In 1988, after the gassing of civilians during Iraq's Kurdistan offensive, a well-supported sanctions bill had foundered on opposition from the White House. Despite the Iraqi regime's excesses, documented in the United States by the Washington-based Middle East Watch organization, the Bush administration maintained an indulgent view of the Iraqi dictator. Saddam had somehow avoided inclusion in the American demonology occupied by Castro, Gaddafi and the successors of Ayatollah Khomeini.

This indulgence was fostered by influential right wing think-tanks and academics who admired the solidity of Saddam's Baathist regime and its proven anti-fundamentalist credentials. Concern about Saddam, where it existed, centred on his efforts to acquire nuclear and missile technology which might at some stage present a threat, not to his Gulf neighbours, but to Israel.

Britain took a more jaundiced view of the Iraqi dictator than did the Americans. The trial and execution of Farzad Bazoft, an Iranian-born London-based journalist alleged to have spied on Iraqi military installations during an official press trip to Iraq in 1989, had stretched relations to breaking point and focused public attention on the human rights record of Saddam's regime. So had the so-called 'supergun' affair in which, in the spring of 1990, British customs officials impounded sections of a huge artillery piece being manufactured in Britain on Iraq's behalf.

But the unexpected freeing of Bazoft's co-defendant, Daphne Parish, on 16 July, after she had served only six months of a fifteen-year sentence for spying, was interpreted as a sign of improved Iraqi behaviour and an augury of better relations. Britain was keen to maintain relations for economic and political reasons despite its distaste for the Iraqi regime. At the time of the Bazoft trial, an important British credit line aimed at securing Iraqi business had been up for tender and, on the political front, the foreign secretary, Douglas Hurd, noted that a break with Iraq would mean that Britain had no diplomatic representation between the Khyber Pass and the Mediterranean, given the lack of relations with Syria and Iran and the closure of its embassy in Kabul.

With some reservations, therefore, the United States and Britain were prepared to accept Iraq for what it had appeared to be two years earlier at the end of the war with Iran – a state weakened by eight years of conflict which now intended to concentrate on domestic reconstruction. The central crisis in the Middle East, according to the Western analysis, was the continued stalemate in the Arab–Israeli conflict, which by the spring of 1990 appeared to have been exacerbated by the formation of a hardline Likud government in Israel. If Iraq was perceived as a threat, it was as a power which was muddying the waters by issuing threats against Israel just at a time when the West was increasing its own diplomatic pressure on that state. The real threat from Iraq – that directed against the conservative regimes of the Arab Gulf – was ignored.

The year following the Gulf ceasefire saw the collapse of Soviet satellite regimes in eastern Europe, the destruction of the Berlin

Wall and the accelerating disintegration of Communist hegemony in the Soviet Union itself. Western liberal democracy appeared to have triumphed. The debate in Washington was whether, in this new political climate, the United States still had a superpower role. No one, certainly not George Bush – or even Saddam Hussein – would have predicted, in the week before the Kuwait invasion, that the United States was about to reassert that role more forcefully than at any time since the Vietnam war.

That it did so was the result of mutual miscalculation: the West failed to perceive the threat, and Iraq underestimated the likely Western response to its aggression. Signals from both sides were either misleading or misinterpreted. The West regarded Iraq's arms build-up and its attempted acquisition of high-tech weapons as a worrying but essentially long-term threat to Israel. Saddam interpreted the West's conciliatory statements, and its lack of urgency in developing a new strategy for Gulf security after the Iran–Iraq war, as signs of indifference about the fate of the Gulf's weaker states.

These misconceptions led to a monumental failure of intelligence and analysis on the Western side. Even when Iraq had massed 100,000 troops on the Kuwaiti border in the days before the invasion, the interpretation put forward by Western intelligence agencies and accepted by their governments was that Baghdad was indulging in traditional Middle Eastern minatory diplomacy with a view to wringing financial concessions from the Kuwaitis. Iraq's traditional claims on Kuwaiti territory were well known but few believed that Saddam would pursue them to their logical conclusion and undertake a full-scale invasion so soon after a debilitating eight-year war.

This analysis reflected a failure by Western governments to understand the ideological nature of both the Baathist regime in Baghdad and its leader. Saddam was viewed with distaste because of his ruthless treatment of his domestic opponents, his gassing of the Kurds and his conduct of the war against Iran. But he was seen basically as a petty tyrant whose human rights abuses followed a pattern regrettably well established in the Third World. Saddam's saving grace, his apologists in the West argued, was that he could guarantee stability in a state which possessed the largest oil reserves in the world outside Saudi Arabia – this despite the evidence of internal corruption and chronic economic misman-agement.

This Western analysis overlooked the expansionist nature of Saddam's Baathist regime and dismissed his self-declared intention to be master of the Gulf and leader of the Arab world. Western commentators viewed him as an essentially Middle Eastern pheno-menon, and rejected comparisons with Hitler as naive. And yet the Baathist doctrine which Saddam espoused shared ideological roots with European fascism. Its totalitarian pan-Arabism was a mirror image of Hitler's pan-Germanism. Under Saddam the Baathists adopted a cult of violence which was closer to Nazism than to the arbitrary despotism which had been practised in the Middle East. With hindsight it might seem obvious that Baathist Iraq was a threat to world peace. But this was not the prevailing view before the summer of 1990.

Saddam's assessment of the consequences of his aggression was equally ill-conceived. His responses in the early weeks of the crisis displayed a tendency, already apparent in the Gulf war, to pursue a campaign without planning a coherent strategy. Had he con-tented himself with occupying the disputed islands of Bubiyan and Warbah and that sector of the Rumeileh oilfield which he claimed as his own, it is unlikely that the United Nations would have gone beyond the imposition of unenforceable sanctions, or that the United States would have dispatched a single soldier to the region. He also misjudged the reaction of the world community, including his fellow Arab leaders. Had a puppet government been left in charge of a nominally independent Kuwait, it would eventually have received some recognition, at least from the Arab world.

Saddam appeared to have been convinced by his own rhetoric that he had become, through the Gulf war, the natural leader of the Arab world and a focus for the aspirations of the Arab masses who would surely rise up against their rulers if these sided with the West. And he underrated the changed international situation in which the United States could lead a major military and diplomatic counter-offensive without being constrained by the fear of a conflict with the Soviet Union.

In 1980, when Saddam's forces had marched into Iran, the international response had been minimal. It took the Security Council several days to formulate a resolution which, while calling for a ceasefire, failed to demand the withdrawal of Iraqi forces or to condemn Iraq for its aggression. But his target in 1980 had been a pariah regime which the United States itself had actively sought to dislodge; to that extent his invasion of Iran had tacit American approval. Superpower relations were also at a low point in 1980 following the Soviet invasion of Afghanistan.

In January 1980, one month after the Soviet invasion of Afghanistan, the then US president had enunciated the so-called Carter doctrine: 'Any attempt by any outside force to gain control of the Persian Gulf will be regarded as an assault on the vital interests of the United States of America and such an assault will be repelled by any means necessary, including military force.' The threat was aimed at the Soviet Union which, it was feared, might take advantage of the post-revolutionary turmoil in Iran to intervene there. A few days before Iraq invaded Iran on 22 September 1980, President Carter's Special Co-ordination Committee met in Washington to discuss reports of a Soviet troop build-up along the Iranian frontier. In the course of discussions involving Carter, Secretary of State Edmund Muskie, Defence Secretary Harold Brown and the national security adviser, Zbigniew Brzezinski, the Committee concluded that, as the United States did not have the forces in the area to mount a conventional military response, the only possible option in the event of Soviet intervention was a nuclear attack. This realization acted as a powerful restraint on US policy.

The situation in 1990 was quite different. Kuwait was a state which had neither the means nor the desire to threaten Iraq (a charge levelled against Iran to justify the 1980 invasion). It was clearly an innocent victim in terms of international law. Furthermore, the Soviet Union's retreat from the international scene, together with its desire for good relations with Washington, meant Moscow did nothing to restrain the US response and, in fact, actively supported it in the Security Council from the first day of the invasion.

The motives behind the former US indulgence towards Iraq are not difficult to discern. The overriding concern of American policy both before and during the Gulf war was to prevent any Soviet advance, either diplomatic or military, into the region. The fall of the Shah in 1979 and his replacement by a vehemently anti-American Islamic regime had created the additional necessity of preventing the Iranian revolution spreading beyond its borders, particularly to the vulnerable Western-oriented states of the southern Gulf, such as Saudi Arabia, Bahrain and the United Arab Emirates.

For the two decades following the overthrow of the Iraqi monarchy in 1958, Iraq was ruled by a succession of radical, anti-Western regimes. From 1967, the year of the Arab–Israeli six-day war, until 1984, Iraq and the United States had no formal diplomatic relations. From the mid-1970s, however, and particularly after the outbreak of the Gulf war in 1980, both sides worked to change this. Iraq, which in American eyes had taken on the image of a Soviet surrogate, gradually came to be seen as a useful ally in the battle against Islamic fundamentalism. In fact, the mutual decision to renew formal ties was made in 1980, shortly before the war began, but was postponed until 1984, in Saddam's words, 'to avoid misinterpretation'.

The rapprochement was momentarily disrupted in 1986 by the Irangate scandal, the secret American arms-for-hostages deal with Tehran. This arose from the White House's desire to reach an accommodation with the Iranians at the same time as it was cultivating the Iraqis and thereby to maintain a balance of power between the warring parties in the Gulf. After Irangate, however, there was a marked switch in US policy towards Iraq. A decision by the United States in 1987 to put the oil tankers of Iraq's then ally, Kuwait, under the protection of the American flag led to an increased US military presence in the Gulf, effectively on Iraq's side. There were clashes with the Iranian navy, Iranian off-shore oil installations were attacked and in July 1988, the cruiser *USS*

Vincennes shot down an Iran Air airliner, killing all 290 people aboard. Iran interpreted the incident as a signal that the United States was preparing a large-scale offensive against it. Two weeks later, Tehran accepted a ceasefire with Iraq under the terms of UN Security Council resolution 598.

Iraq emerged from the Gulf war as ostensibly moderate. Gone were the pro-Soviet pronouncements and the radical rhetoric. Saddam Hussein was perceived as a reasonable man who shared the Western consensus on the need to maintain stability and the status quo in the Gulf now the war was over.

This perception was to be modified in the next two years as evidence emerged of Iraq's repression of the Kurds and its use of chemical weapons against them. Baghdad's procrastination in negotiating a peace treaty with Iran on the basis of resolution 598 gave rise to widespread doubts about Iraqi intentions, and Washington was aware of Iraq's renewed intimidation of Kuwait and its attempts to secure rights to the two Kuwaiti islands of Bubiyan and Warbah. Assurances were privately given to Kuwait of US support if it were attacked. But despite the unease felt in some quarters of the new Bush administration, Washington's response to Iraqi excesses always fell short of outright condemnation. American and other Western officials were all too ready to accept Saddam's view that his negative image was the result of a press campaign orchestrated by Iraq's enemies.

When a bipartisan US delegation visited Saddam Hussein on 12 April 1990 to express concern both about Iraq's development of chemical, biological and nuclear weapons and about the recent threats against Israel, much of the discussion involved the role of the Western press. Senator Alan Simpson explained to Saddam, according to the Iraqi account of the meeting: 'Democracy is a difficult thing. I think the troubles you have are with the Western media, not with the American government. The press is full of itself . . . They take themselves for wise politicians, geniuses. All journalists.'

Most of the senators in the delegation were from grain states which, because of the importance of US grain exports to Iraq, had a particular interest in the threatened imposition of sanctions. Six months after the meeting between Saddam and the senators a record of the proceedings had yet to be written into the congressional record. The Iraqis, however, had bugged the room and were able to make available a transcript in Baghdad in a volume presciently entitled *The Confrontation*.

In the exchanges with Senators Bob Dole, Alan Simpson, Howard Mitzenbaum, and James McClure, Saddam showed himself to be particularly sensitive about a broadcast on 15 February by the Voice of America which had compared his regime, among others, with the fallen Communist regimes of eastern Europe. 'The success of dictatorial rule and tyranny,' the VOA commentator had said, 'requires the existence of a large secret police force, while the success of democracy requires abolishment of such a force.' The broadcast spoke of thousands of Romanian citizens shedding their blood to bring down the Ceauşescu regime 'against well-trained security forces armed to the teeth'. It went on to say that secret police were still widely present in states such as China, North Korea, Iran, Iraq, Syria, Libya, Cuba and Albania, before concluding: 'We believe that the 1990s should belong not to the dictators and secret police, but to the people.'

The broadcast, which Saddam understood to represent the views of the US government (with some justification, given its source), was the main ground for his complaint to the senators that 'a vast campaign has been launched against us in America and in the countries of Europe'. Dole replied: 'It doesn't come from President Bush. He told us yesterday he was against all that.' He later added somewhat gratuitously that 'a person who was not authorized to speak in the name of the government, a commentator of the Voice of America – which represents the government – has been removed'.

The VOA broadcast had earlier been the subject of a formal complaint by Baghdad when the US ambassador, April Glaspie, was called in by the foreign minister, Tareq Aziz, to receive a protest against a 'flagrant interference in the internal affairs of Iraq'.

Ms Glaspie cabled the State Department that the Iraqi regime saw the VOA broadcast as government-sanctioned 'mud-slinging with the intent to incite revolution'. The supposed analogy to Romania had been 'deeply damaging'. And, in a phrase guaranteed to provoke a frisson in Washington even in early 1990, she wrote: 'The Soviet embassy is also busy here ensuring that news of the editorial has been spread throughout Baghdad.'

She subsequently wrote to Aziz that: 'It is absolutely not United States policy to question the legitimacy of the government of Iraq nor to interfere in any way in the domestic concerns of the Iraqi people and government. My government regrets that the wording of the editorial left it open to incorrect interpretation.' Back in Washington, the US Information Agency was told that in order to prevent future embarrassment VOA editorials should henceforth have prior written clearance from the State Department.

Against this background of apparent appeasement, and also against the background of Iraq's increasingly bellicose threats to Kuwait, Ambassador Glaspie was summoned to see Saddam Hussein at one o'clock on 25 July, one week before the invasion. A transcript of the meeting was later leaked by the Iraqis and, although State Department officials played down the significance of the conversation and suggested the Iraqi version was incomplete, the authenticity of the transcript has not been challenged.

In it, Saddam makes it clear that a conflict could result from his dispute with Kuwait; he further warns that the United States should not get involved; he then receives an assurance from Ms Glaspie that Washington regards the dispute as an inter-Arab affair which the United States would like to see solved by the Arabs themselves.

'We have no opinion on Arab–Arab conflicts, like your border disagreement with Kuwait,' the ambassador is quoted as saying. While this hardly expressed American approval for Iraqi aggression, Saddam may have gained the impression that Washington would be unlikely to intervene. Certainly, Ms Glaspie failed to rise to Saddam's overtly threatening remarks during the course of the meeting, and he may have interpreted her diplomatic reluctance to argue with a head of state as an indication that she accepted his case.

In what Saddam said was intended as a message to President Bush, he argued that, of course, America was free to choose its own friends in the region – a reference to the conservative Gulf states, including Kuwait. 'But you know you are not the ones who protected your friends during the war with Iran. I assure you, had the Iranians overrun the region, American troops would not have stopped them, except by the use of nuclear weapons.'

Saddam was aware that this assessment was valid for 1980 but not for 1990. America's engagement in the Gulf was no longer constrained by the threat of nuclear confrontation with the Soviet Union. Saddam had already warned his fellow Arabs that the end of the Cold War presented a danger to the Arab world. He now spelt out to Ms Glaspie the consequences of conventional war, should America decide to intervene.

'Yours is a society which cannot accept 10,000 dead in one battle . . . we know that you can harm us although we do not threaten you. But we can harm you. Everyone can cause harm according to their ability and their size,' Saddam said. He went on to add the threat of terrorist action in the event of war: 'We cannot come all the way to you in the United States but individual Arabs may reach you.'

'You can come to Iraq with aircraft and missiles but do not push us to the point where we cease to care. And when we feel that you want to injure our pride and take the Iraqis' chance of a high standard of living, then we will cease to care and death will be the choice for us. Then we would not care if you fired one hundred missiles for each missile we fired. Because without pride, life would have no value.'

Iraq did not, of course, place the United States among its enemies, he went on to assure Ms Glaspie, and a solution to the dispute with Kuwait must naturally be sought within an Arab framework. 'We don't want war because we know what war means. But do not push us to consider war as the only solution to live proudly and to provide our people with a good living. We know that the United States has nuclear weapons but we are determined either to live as proud men or we will die.'

In his message to President Bush, Saddam told the ambassador he had evidence that certain elements linked with the US State Department and the intelligence community were attempting to turn the conservative Gulf states against Iraq and persuade them to withhold economic aid from Iraq. (He did not accuse Bush and the secretary of state, James Baker, of participation in such a campaign.) 'Iraq came out of the war burdened with $40 billion debts, excluding the aid given by Arab states, some of which consider that too to be a debt, although they knew – and you knew too – that without Iraq they would not have had these sums and the future of the region would have been entirely different.'

And again Saddam showed his obsession with the alleged campaign by the 'official' American media with an apparent reference to the Voice of America broadcast. 'The United States thought that the situation in Iraq was like Poland, Romania or Czechoslovakia. We were disturbed by this campaign but we were not disturbed too much because we had hoped that, in a few months, those who are decision-makers in America would have a chance to find the facts and see whether this media campaign had had any effect on the lives of Iraqis.'

The ambassador was conciliatory in her response, pointing out that the administration had rejected the idea of trade sanctions against Iraq and noting that an apology had already been issued for the offending editorial. 'I am pleased that you add your voice to the diplomats who stand up to the media,' she said. 'If the American president had control of the media, his job would be much easier.'

President Bush, she assured Saddam, wanted better and deeper relations with Iraq and also an Iraqi contribution to peace and prosperity in the Middle East. 'President Bush is an intelligent man,' said Ms Glaspie. 'He is not going to declare an economic war against Iraq.'

The ambassador went on to express her personal admiration for Saddam's 'extraordinary efforts' to rebuild Iraq, adding: 'I know you need funds.' She then reaffirmed that the United States had no opinion on the Kuwait border issue. 'I was in the American embassy in Kuwait during the late sixties,' said Ms Glaspie. 'The instruction we had during this period was that we should express no opinion on this issue and that the issue is not associated with America. James Baker has directed our official spokesman to emphasize this instruction.'

Despite this, Ms Glaspie said that she had been instructed 'in the spirit of friendship' to determine Iraq's intentions. Saddam replied that it was natural and proper that the United States should be concerned when peace was at issue. 'But what we ask is not to express your concern in a way that would make an aggressor believe that he is getting support for his aggression.' The aggressor, in this context, was Kuwait, which stood accused by Saddam of pushing down the world oil price, thereby threatening the livelihoods of Iraqis, 'harming even the milk our children drink and the pension of the widow who lost a husband during the war and the pensions of the orphans who lost their parents'.

The Kuwaitis had lied and dissembled, gone back on their word, broken agreements, Saddam pronounced. Nevertheless, there was still a chance for peace. Saddam revealed that he had agreed with President Hosni Mubarak of Egypt that there would be a high-level meeting in Saudi Arabia between Iraq and Kuwait. 'He just telephoned me a short while ago to say the Kuwaitis have agreed to that suggestion.'

'This is good news. Congratulations,' said Ms Glaspie.

Saddam gave a final warning that 'if we are unable to find a solution, then it will be natural that Iraq will not accept death.'

Ms Glaspie told Saddam that, in view of the tension between Iraq and Kuwait, she had been thinking of postponing a scheduled trip to Washington, but after their discussions she would now travel on 30 July with the intention of speaking to President Bush. She flew out of Baghdad on the following Monday. Three days later Iraq invaded Kuwait.

April Glaspie, a forty-eight-year-old career diplomat, with wide experience of the Arab world, subsequently defended herself in an interview with the *New York Times* against the charge that she had failed to read the signals coming from the Iraqis. 'Obviously I didn't think and nobody else did, that the Iraqis were going to take all of Kuwait. Every Kuwaiti and Saudi, every analyst in the Western world was wrong too. That does not excuse me. But people who now claim that all was clear were not heard from at the time.'

The use of the phrase 'all of Kuwait' was significant. Did it imply that, had Saddam confined his incursion to the border area and to the disputed islands, the United States might have eventually accepted the new status quo?

Certainly Washington recognized that some change in the Middle East was likely in response to the ending of the Cold War. Yet as the barriers had crumbled in eastern Europe a year earlier the Arabs had only watched in wonder. In the Middle East, there was nothing comparable to the radical restructuring which went on across eastern Europe, no sudden realization that their emperors wore no clothes or that people had the power to change governments. Kuwait, alone in the Gulf, seemed touched by the new spirit of democracy: opposition groups there were emboldened to step up their protests and demand a return at least to the partial democracy they had experienced in the past when a National Assembly, within carefully defined limits, was allowed to examine and criticize the policies of the state and the conduct of its ministers.

In Iraq, the most powerful and the most repressive dictatorship of all, the overthrow of Communism in eastern Europe, the restructuring of the Soviet Union and the end of the Cold War had little impact, not least because there was far less coverage of these events in the newspapers or on television. This was hardly surprising in a country where the state controls all information media, where ownership of even a typewriter has to be registered, and possession of a duplicating machine means constant police surveillance.

So as the superpowers met to determine their new roles after the revolutions of 1989, there was one problem which was constantly raised, and regularly put aside. While other conflicts in which superpower rivalry had played a central role – Afghanistan, Cambodia, Nicaragua – moved closer to settlement, one remained intractable: the Middle East. The central issue, of course, and the one which occupied most time at the meetings between James Baker and Eduard Shevardnadze, the American and Soviet foreign ministers, was the Arab–Israeli dispute, a crisis which had lasted since 1948 and which showed no signs of disappearing.

Yet, as the months went on and the contacts multiplied, there was a gradual coming together of the two sides; the Soviets modified their support of the more militant Arab states and their opposition to Israel, while the Americans began to mend fences with the radical Arab countries and to look more critically at Israel's actions and its constant requests for more financial and military help.

The American ambassador, who was withdrawn over the attempted bombing of the El-Al airliner in London in 1986, returned to Damascus just as the Soviet Union warned Syria's President Hafez al-Assad that in future he would have to make out a good case for all the hardware he wanted, that he would have to pay for it in real money, and that his dream of reaching strategic parity with Israel would have to be abandoned. Jews were being allowed out of Russia in numbers which meant that the population of Israel might double by the end of the century, while America insisted that none of the new immigrants should settle in the occupied West Bank.

Gradually, the two superpowers seemed to be working out a modus vivendi in the Middle East, which meant that sooner or later their client states would also have to find new positions, to end old rivalries and remove current threats.

The Kuwait crisis erupted as a new world order was emerging but before the old patterns of confrontation, at least in the Middle East, had been replaced by those of co-operation. The collapse of Soviet power, so widely welcomed in the West, exposed the vast national differences in political development which would complicate the birth of the new order. While Europe, for instance, was moving towards greater integration, the peoples of the Soviet Union were rediscovering a regional nationalism which had been suppressed for seventy years. In the Middle East an even more anachronistic tendency was manifested by the imperialist aspirations of Saddam Hussein.

At the very moment when the world was burying the legacy of the Second World War, symbolized by the unification of Germany and the preparations for a Soviet–German treaty, Saddam rose up to spoil the celebrations. He was an old-fashioned expansionist dictator, and the world chose to confront him with the old conventional military means. The perception that sanctions alone would not work against him soon became the watchword of the leaders of the anti-Saddam alliance; the only alternative, therefore, was war or the threat of war.

Before the crisis, the main political threat to the new world order was thought to be the unpredictable effects of the imminent break-up of the Soviet Union though even this had begun to take second place to global concerns about the environment, drugs and the imbalances of international trade. Before the crisis, it seemed as if the new order would be dominated by the new economic powers – Germany, Japan, and the Asian states of the Pacific rim. But faced with Saddam's threat, it was the old Western military powers, the United States, Britain and France, which took the lead in containing him.

If it had been an error to ignore Saddam's superpower pre-tensions in the past, it would have been an even graver error to ignore the danger he now represented. Among those who opposed a military solution were some who argued that the West itself, by arming Saddam and supporting his war against Iran, had created a Frankenstein monster – as if to suggest that it was hypocritical to attempt, however belatedly, to halt the monster's rampage.

Others claimed that it was morally reprehensible to try to stifle the attempts of a third world state to acquire all the available benefits of modern technology. Less than one month before the invasion, a senior consultant to a major British weapons' manufac-turer suggested to the present authors in the urbane surroundings of London's Reform Club that their fear that Saddam might one day have nuclear weapons was nothing short of 'racialist'.

Saddam himself would surely have shared this opinion; for where was it written that the world would always be dominated by the existing powers? Who had decreed that the Arabs must live eternally within colonially imposed borders when, in the West, the very map of Europe was being redrawn?

In the final analysis, the strength of the international response to Saddam's challenge was not about Kuwait or the future security of Israel or even about oil; it was about the status of the existing powers – particularly of the United States – in the new world order. The threat of nuclear war between the superpowers might have receded but, as Saddam Hussein himself believed, military power still seemed the decisive factor in world affairs. This was not to say that the United States engineered the crisis, although talk of a US–Iraqi plot to dominate the Gulf soon emerged as one of the more bizarre products of the Middle Eastern conspiracy mill.

Responsibility for the crisis lay with Saddam Hussein. His invasion was a gamble, a challenge to the world which, if ignored, would surely lead to worse disasters. By 1990, Iraq had embarked on a weapons programme which would eventually give it nuclear parity with Israel (no bad thing, according to many Arabs). And while Iraq had short-term economic problems, it was potentially a big power. At the end of the Gulf war it had, in terms of available manpower, the fourth largest army in the world, and the missiles it was developing were capable of reaching southern Europe. After the invasion of Kuwait, warnings of Iraq's future military capacity and intentions suddenly appeared less apocalyptic than before.

Even those countries which had played the greatest part in allowing Saddam to build up his power were forced to join the alliance designed to contain him. France, which looked to the Gulf for 31 per cent of its imports, (15 per cent of its total energy requirements) had built up a special relationship with Iraq during the Gulf war. The invasion therefore presented France with a particular dilemma; yet it was swift to condemn what had happened. And though it appeared slow to commit itself to action, this was, in fact, a misleading perception, caused by the publicity given to the contrary voices raised in the French government. France actually committed more men and ships than any country except the United States in the first weeks of the crisis, and was quick to move its naval force to the region.

However, at the same time, President Mitterrand seemed less than totally committed to the American-led crusade. At the end of October he appeared to break ranks when, in a UN speech, he linked an Iraqi withdrawal from Kuwait with the convening of an international conference to settle all Middle East problems, including the Arab–Israeli issue. President Bush was forced to follow up the French initiative, emphasizing that there had to be a total and unconditional withdrawal. Douglas Hurd, the British foreign secretary, also weighed in with a similar speech. All three said basically the same thing, though Bush and Hurd tried to blur the link which Mitterrand made.

In several Asian countries too, views were less black and white than those taken in the United States or in much of Europe. India, Bangladesh, Sri Lanka, Pakistan and the Philippines all had large numbers of their nationals in Kuwait and in Iraq itself; their concern about the fate of those people modified their rhetoric at the UN and determined their actions. India, for instance, took the lead in the campaign to exploit the loophole in the UN sanctions resolution which allowed food and medicines to be sent to an embargoed country 'for humanitarian reasons'. Other states in the Far East decided to send troops to join the alliance against Iraq: Pakistan, with historic links with Saudi Arabia and with Iran, was one of the first countries to commit forces, then, rather surprisingly, Bangladesh joined in – and was handsomely rewarded with aid from Saudi Arabia.

Japan, like Germany, was barred from sending troops by the constitution forced on it by the Western allies at the end of the 1939–45 war but, with its world-dominating economy, it was nonetheless expected to put up much of the finance needed. It did so with some initial reluctance, only doubling its first offer of $1 billion after considerable American and European pressure (though soon after it doubled the amount again). A government proposal that volunteer non-combatant forces should be sent to the Gulf was rejected by the Japanese parliament.

Japanese public interest was conditioned by the plight of the more than 200 Japanese living in Kuwait who took refuge in their country's embassy and were accommodated in a spacious basement in the building. The Ambassador was away, and after some pressure from the Iraqis, the chargé d'affaires decided that since the Baghdad government had announced it no longer recognized the presence of any embassies in Kuwait, it would be better for the Japanese in the embassy building to surrender and go to Baghdad, in the hope of repatriation. Instead, all the Japanese were taken hostage. This created a wave of criticism from the Japanese media and public, and the unfortunate chargé was warned by the Japanese Foreign Ministry not to return to Tokyo even if the Iraqis allowed him to leave the country.

The Soviet Union was equally concerned about its citizens in Iraq, it also had the problem of having 193 military experts with the Iraqi armed forces – the Soviet command was careful to emphasize that they had no 'military advisers' in Iraq but 'military experts' – technicians who were putting into service some of the more sophisticated equipment sold by the Soviet Union to Iraq; it was the sort of after-sales service which any company provided, they said blandly. Lt.-Gen. Vladimir Nikitiuk, deputy head of the supply department of the High Command, spelt it out: 'The 193 experts are commanded by Maj.-Gen. Anatoly Bannikov. They have never had anything to do with organizational issues in the Iraqi armed forces, nor with the planning of combat operations, nor with combat training for either men or officers. This applies to both the Iran–Iraq conflict and to the present day.'

The Soviet military experts in Iraq were the ones who received most publicity, but there were another fifty experts and their families in Kuwait on 2 August, as well as 830 other Soviet nationals; in Iraq, in addition to the military personnel, there were more than 7,500 Soviet citizens. All these people were of concern to the Soviet Union. But it was the presence of the military which most affected policy: several 'Soviet generals publicly acknowledged that it was difficult for them to change course, and suddenly to look on Iraq as an aggressor and potential enemy, when they had been working with the armed forces of that country for more than twenty years. Indeed, Soviet advisers were present in Iraq even before the fifteen-year Treaty of Friendship and Co-operation was concluded between the two countries in 1972. Certainly the Iraqis believed that the Soviet general staff exerted a moderating influence on the politicians. In Baghdad, officials told us that they had their links to Moscow, and they were quite certain that at the Helsinki summit in mid-September the influence of Soviet military thinking made Gorbachev hold back from any endorsement of military action against Iraq if sanctions proved ineffective. Whether or not this was true, the Iraqis firmly believed that it was and that the Soviet generals would prevent any attack on them. This perception undoubtedly influenced the Baghdad government's policy of brinkmanship.

Another important element in Iraq's role as aggressor was Saddam's ambition to become the new Nasser. Regardless of the truth, he saw himself as the victor in the war with Iran. In fact the conflict had been brought to an end by the increasing effectiveness of the embargo against Iran – the American-led Operation Staunch, the stubborn defence of their homeland by the Shia soldiers of the Iraqi army who put nationalism above religious solidarity, and the command of the Gulf sea lanes by American warships, which had forced Ayatollah Khomeini to accept the UN ceasefire resolution. But Iraq believed that it alone had brought about the Iranian 'capitulation', and this fed Saddam Hussein's delusions of grandeur: he was to become the new leader of the Arab world. And he knew that the only way to fulfil this ambition was to be accepted as the champion of Palestine.

Yet Saddam was no fool; he did not want to have to take on Israel in battle – apart from anything else, Iraq has no common border with Israel, and neither Syria nor Jordan would take kindly to their territory being used as a battleground. He planned to make himself the acknowledged champion and mentor of the PLO, so that it would be to him that the Palestinian people looked, rather than the other Arab leaders who had so signally failed them. Saddam Hussein saw himself as the liberator of Palestine, but he planned to achieve this by the threat of war, not by war itself. He realized that Israel's weakness was its inability to take casualties: Israel could win a war, but it could not survive as a viable state with thousands of people killed, most of them civilians. There would be mass emigration and no new immigrants. This recognition coloured the strategies of both sides. While Israel was determined to prevent Iraq acquiring nuclear weapons, and wanted the overthrow of Saddam Hussein, the Iraqis were eager to demonstrate their possession of chemical weapons and rockets powerful enough to reach Israel.

Saddam recognized that in order to achieve his ambitions he needed a stable base and a country rich enough to arm itself. Oil could give him the necessary wealth, but if the oil revenues were not to be mortgaged for years to come, setting back his more grandiose programmes, the debts of the eight war years had to be written off. With the Iraqi army still mobilized and no peace treaty between the antagonists, so that Iraq's control of the Gulf was still threatened by Iran, Saudi Arabia had willingly agreed to Iraqi demands that the huge loans made between 1980 and 1988 should be turned into outright grants. Saudi Arabia could afford it, and the reward was a treaty of non-aggression from Iraq, which let the ever-fearful Saudi princes sleep a little more soundly in their beds.

The Kuwaitis were made of sterner stuff. They had surprised the world with their Thatcher-style response to aircraft hijackings and hostage-taking: they just would not negotiate. Even when it emerged during a 1988 hijacking of a Kuwaiti airliner that a relative of the ruler was among those held, the Kuwaitis still would not bargain with the hijackers. And for all the public threats and behind-the-scenes approaches made, they rebuffed all attempts to rescue seventeen men they had imprisoned for terrorism, even refusing a visa for Terry Waite when he tried to secure their release in exchange for the hostages in Beirut he was soon to join.

The end of the war with Iran brought little immediate benefit to the people of Iraq. Saddam was aware that discontent was simmering not far below the surface. Demobilized soldiers were unable to find jobs, and often reacted violently against Egyptian immigrants who had taken their places. There was a crime-wave and the security services reported more open criticism than ever before. Saddam was determined to avoid a repetition of the events in eastern Europe. (Some of his closest associates said they had been shown videos of the executions of the Ceauşescus in Romania, with the warning that if anything similar happened in Iraq, history demonstrated that the leader would not be the only one to face the anger of the people.) Iraq needed a new rallying point.

Kuwait fitted the bill perfectly: it had been depressing the oil price by over-production; it had refused to write off the debts owed by Iraq; there was a long-standing territorial dispute which could act as a pretext and which would also be popular among the Iraqi people; and the nature of the regime in Kuwait was such that little sympathy for the country might be expected. But for the swift and firm response of George Bush, things might have gone Saddam's way, for the Arab reaction on the day of the invasion was fumbling and uncertain. Without the strong lead given by the Americans, Iraq might have got away with it. News of the invasion was actually withheld for days by Saudi Arabia and the other states of the Arabian peninsula. Although it was quickly the talk of the souks in every country, all information had to be obtained from the BBC, Voice of America, or Monte Carlo radios.

If, in those first days, Saudi Arabia or some other powerful Arab government had sought to minimize the Iraqi action or to ensure it was treated as a purely Arab affair, Saddam might have achieved what he set out to do – to occupy the whole of Kuwait as a prelude to a settlement which would have left him in control of those parts he really wanted. Given a general Arab willingness to negotiate, Saddam would have accepted a Kuwaiti government under Iraqi control – a rump state, but still one of the richest places on earth, and well able to compensate its puppet rulers for their lack of real power.

Even the Arab countries which soon joined the American alliance against Iraq would have hesitated to act if they had not been given a firm lead: Syria alone would have been certain to oppose Saddam's action, and given the record of Syrian–Iraqi hostility, would have had little impact.

Saddam acknowledged later that the swift American response had influenced his subsequent strategy. He told Bulent Ecevit, the former Turkish Prime Minister: 'Kuwait is now ours, but we might have refrained from taking such a decision if US troops were not massed in the region with the threat of invading us.'

Saddam said if the US had not sent troops, Iraq 'would have attempted to develop the status of the temporary revolutionary administration' set up in Kuwait after the 2 August invasion. He told Ecevit that the revolutionary group was not strong enough to stand up to the American force. 'We would not have been able to ask our people and the armed forces to fight to the last drop of blood if we had not said that Kuwait was now part of Iraq. We would not have been able to prepare our people for the possibility of war.'

And there was another practical reason that Saddam did not specify: the so-called 'provisional government' was a sham, as the Iraqis could find no Kuwaitis willing to join it.

Throughout the world, the strong initiative from Washington made all the difference. In Europe, Britain was the first to respond, and was always strongest in its support of President Bush – the principle of opposing anything that looked like unprovoked aggression was dear to the heart of Mrs Thatcher, and she drew clear analogies with the Argentine invasion of the Falklands in 1982. She also recognized the political advantage in giving wholehearted backing to Bush: there would be an election in Britain by 1992 at the latest, the Tories were trailing in the polls, and previous experience had shown that a small war did a power of good for a Conservative government.

Elsewhere in Europe there was a quicker appreciation that the fight with Iraq might not be a small war. In Germany, Chancellor Helmut Kohl deplored the section of the German constitution which made it impossible for him to send troops to the Gulf, and said he was determined to change it; months later, however, nothing had been done. Bonn was far too occupied with arranging the merger between East and West Germany to pay much attention to foreign adventures, and unlike Britain, saw no advantage in becoming involved – apart, of course, from the acknowledged need to demonstrate that a large and powerful state should not be allowed to take over a weak neighbour.

Before the invasion of Kuwait, a number of academics with experience of the Gulf had taken a less sanguine view of Iraq than did government officials. The academics recognized that the threat of Iraqi expansionism had not been removed simply by Iraq's failure to secure a swift victory in the conflict with Iran. Towards the end of the war, one of them, Hermann F. Eilts, a former US ambassador to Saudi Arabia and Egypt, wrote:

> Should Iraq win, or should the war end with the Iraqi military machine still reasonably intact, Kuwaitis fear that they might again be pressured by their stronger neighbour for total subservience or territorial concessions. At a minimum, the protracted negotiations prior to the Iran–Iraq war over Iraq's demand for the Kuwaiti islands of Warbah and Bubiyan would doubtless have to be resolved quickly in Iraq's favour. Kuwait obviously hopes that by providing financial and other support for Iraq, it is buying the latter's goodwill. But goodwill is an effervescent commodity in Gulf politics, as it is in international politics anywhere and as the Kuwaitis well know.

Eighteen months after the war was over, another academic, Gerd Nonneman, also acknowledged the problem of Iraq's claim against Kuwait, but nevertheless added his voice to the consensus when he told a London conference that 'the probability of a return to regional radicalism is extremely low. Nor is Iraq likely to be the bully it used to be'. However, he added a powerful proviso: any analysis of the future of the region, he said, had to be made on the assumption that Saddam remained in power.

> If Saddam does stay in power in the 1990s, a second assumption is that he will continue to act rationally; in other words, that his mental make-up does not give way to the phenomenon which has

affected other long-term dictators, that of living and acting in a universe somewhat removed from reality. Fortunately, this does not seem an immediate prospect: the president, however ruthless, has in the past proved to be politically astute, and to possess a sharp intelligence. Yet the degree to which the personality cult surrounding him has ballooned since the ceasefire, and the specific forms it has taken (leading for instance to persistent rumours he might declare himself king ...) may justify some consideration of that possibility.

Nonneman had hit upon the crucial variable which was to dominate the course of events in the coming months: the character of Saddam Hussein.

The Daring and Aggressive Knight

Some weeks after the invasion of Kuwait, when the US military build-up in Saudi Arabia was already well-advanced, Saddam had a private meeting in Baghdad with the radical Palestinian leader, George Habash. 'It is not Kuwait they want,' he confided to Habash. 'It is me they want. I am the defiant spirit. But I tell them, "before you feed on me, I will feed on you".'

He had intended the conquest of his southern neighbour to challenge the outside world, although he could not predict how it would respond. It was not part of his strategy to start a war with the United States but to establish a new reality in the Gulf which others would be forced to accept and which would bring Iraq one step nearer to becoming the regional superpower.

For a decade and a half Saddam had promoted the concept of a strong modern Arab state which would be the equal of other world powers. He was to be the 'defiant spirit' who would lead the Arabs back to their former glory. His strategy was based on three principles: the acquisition of high technology, the creation of a vast army and rule through terror.

Saddam Hussein al-Takriti was a small-town political gangster who developed an obsession for history, a killer who came to see himself as the reincarnation of the great Arab heroes. Like other Middle Eastern autocrats who attempted to change the order of things – Khomeini in Iran, Gaddafi in Libya – he was dismissed in the West as a madman. In the search for an explanation of Saddam's apparent irrationality in opposing the rest of the world, one Western security service came up with the explanation that the drugs he had recently started taking for angina had had the side effect of giving him a sense of invulnerability. Yet for the previous twenty years he had tortured, murdered and waged war with impunity and few had bothered to assess either his physical or psychological state.

When he took office on 16 July 1979 as President of the Republic of Iraq, his personal and political history was already marked by a trail of blood. It was soon clear that nothing was to change. One of his first official functions was to host a dinner for senior officials of the ruling Arab Baath Socialist Party. The meal at the presidential palace in Baghdad was followed by a meeting of the party leaders at which members were invited to write down details of any meetings they had held in the previous year with two of their colleagues Muhie Abdel-Hussein and Mohamed Ayesh. The following day Saddam chaired a meeting of the Revolutionary Command Council at which it was alleged that these two men were the ringleaders of a Syrian-financed plot to overthrow the regime. On 22 July, Saddam announced to an extraordinary regional conference of the party that he was in a position to supply a full list of the plotters; regrettably it contained the names of some of the highest-ranking members of the regime, including five members – or one quarter – of the Revolutionary Command Council. With tears in his voice, Saddam read out the names of the plotters and asked them to leave the hall.

Some days later, Saddam invited the Baath leadership to accompany him to where their erstwhile comrades were held. And there they were handed guns, and with Saddam at the centre, formed the firing squad which shot them.

According to some accounts, gunmen of the Mukhabarat secret police stood behind the ranks of the executioners lest any should prove recalcitrant. In the event, they all carried out their duty to the party and to their leader. In this way, Saddam established ties of blood and terror with those upon whom he would now rely to enforce his rule.

It was a typical Saddam technique. Instead of following the old Arab tribal convention of ruling by consensus, he opted for the doctrine of shared guilt. In all major issues of state and party, he would make the final decision but others would share the responsibility; it was one of the many tactics he used, apart from terror, to ensure loyalty.

The 1979 purges claimed several hundred lives and annihilated the Baathist old guard which had come to power with Saddam in 1968. Those who died included close colleagues who had been with Saddam throughout his twenty-year struggle for supremacy in the Baath Party. They included Adnan Hussein, a deputy prime minister, considered to be a personal friend of Saddam; Mohamed Ayesh, a leading party organizer; and Ghanin Abdul Jalil, the head of Saddam's old office at the vice-presidency.

The only survivor was the president, Ahmed Hassan al-Bakr, a distant relative of Saddam and a former military officer whose political activity dated back to the 1958 revolution which over-threw the monarchy. But even he was pushed aside by Saddam on the grounds of ill-health. He was put under house arrest and gradually stripped of all his remaining positions. The two men had ruled in tandem for eleven years, with Bakr as president and Sad-dam as his nominal deputy, although it was clear, even to the outside world, that from the mid-1970s, Saddam was the strongman of the regime.

Those who survived were creations of Saddam, either relatives from his hometown of Takrit whom he had raised from his own dirt-poor background or else members of oppressed minorities, such as the Christian, Tareq Aziz, who was to emerge as the ideologue and propagandist of Saddamism.

When he took over the presidency in 1979 Saddam was still only forty-two and he had been active politically for the previous twenty years. His rise to power was based on political cunning but, above all, on an unparalleled ruthlessness. He had spent the decade before he ousted Bakr eliminating anyone who might be a rival, even those who had been life-long friends. According to a former official: 'When you meet him, you quickly realize that he trusts absolutely no one. Everyone is a potential enemy. Some-times you see him with children and he is smiling and stroking their hair. That's because they are no threat to him. But, in order to get his way, even children can become just objects.'

With less intelligence or ambition, Saddam might have ended up as a small-time gangster, a protection racketeer or a hired killer. But in political life, he showed a single-minded dedication to his work – he was routinely at his desk for sixteen or seventeen hours a day – and a shrewd understanding of affairs of state. As vice-president, he successfully masterminded the nationalization of the Iraq Petroleum Company in 1972, showing a firmer grasp of the political and economic complexities of the operation than some of his ablest technocrats.

He rarely travelled abroad and only once to the West (a visit to France in 1975), and yet he was obsessed with acquiring knowledge of Western technology and Western politics. An Arab journalist who went to interview Saddam shortly before the start of the Gulf war was asked to explain how the United States was governed. 'But, your excellency, that will take a long time,' he protested. 'Do you have any other appointment?' Saddam replied ominously. And so the journalist explained the concept of checks and balances, the separation of executive, legislative and judicial functions, until finally Saddam asked: 'Who, then, am I supposed to deal with?'

It was however, for his unwavering ruthlessness that Saddam was best known. He built up a system of state terror to rival those created by Hitler and Stalin. In order to instill fear in the populace, he allowed the secret police to operate an informal rumour mill, ensuring that everyone heard about the brutal consequences of treachery towards the state and its leader. Whenever these reports reached the outside world the regime dismissed them as the inventions of exiles and traitors. It thus became difficult to sort reality from myth.

Western human rights organizations have nevertheless succeeded in assembling a body of evidence which fully justified Saddam's sobriquet, 'Butcher of Baghdad'. Perhaps one of the most damaging indictments of the regime was that issued by Amnesty International in March 1989 which catalogued Iraq's treatment of child detainees and the practice of torturing children in order to extract confessions from their parents. 'Torture of whole groups of children has been recorded,' the report said. 'According to the testimony of a former detainee released from Fusailiyya Security Headquarters in late 1985, some of the 300 children and youths from Sulamaniyeh held at the prison at the time were beaten, whipped, sexually abused and given electric shocks. Three of them were transferred to a military hospital; when they were returned to their cells, one died.'

Amnesty said that some thirty different varieties of torture were in use in Iraqi prisons, ranging from beatings to mutilations. 'Torturers have gouged out the eyes of their victims, cut off their noses, ears, breasts and penises, and axed limbs.'

There is evidence that Saddam Hussein, unlike more fastidious dictators who prefer to leave the dirty work to others, took a direct hand in the repression – certainly as a killer and probably as a torturer as well. During the Gulf war, after the setbacks of 1982 when Iraq's fortunes were at their lowest, Saddam suggested to his ministers that he might step down from the presidency, at least long enough to allow a peace settlement. Most of the Revolutionary Command Council wisely rejected the suggestion but the health minister, the well-respected Riaz Hussein, ventured that Saddam's temporary withdrawal might appease Iran. The president escorted his minister to a private room; there was an argument and voices were raised; Saddam drew his revolver and shot Hussein. According to the version which reached the streets, the dismembered body of the minister was delivered to his wife in a plastic bag.

The Qasr al-Nihayyah – the Palace of the End – was a notorious torture chamber in Baghdad dating from the first bloody Baathist coup in 1963. From 1969 it was presided over by Nadhim Kzar, a psychopathic torturer appointed by Saddam to head the new department of internal state security. An account of an incident there in early 1973 was given to the authors by Abu Ali, the nom de guerre of the European representative of the fundamentalist Shia Daawa movement, who was himself jailed on three occasions and tortured by the regime – for his involvement in the underground anti-Baathist movement. The incident related not to the treatment meted out to Abu Ali, which was horrific enough, but to the torture and murder of a fellow member of Daawa.

At the end of 1972 they arrested an obscure man called Abdu Saheb Dukhail who was shown to be a founder of Daawa,' Abu Ali told us. 'He and another man were taken to Qasr al-Nihayyah where they were tortured so badly by Nadhim Kzar that they were on the point of death. Dukhail confessed, which is the worst mistake, but the other man did not and after years in jail he was freed. What he saw wasn't known about until then. This is a man of great integrity, very meticulous. But he still has nightmares about what he saw. Saddam, who the man knew by sight – he was vice-president, after all – came into the room, picked up Dukhail and dropped him into a bath of acid. And then he watched while the body dissolved.

Violence and brutality had been part of Saddam's life since his earliest childhood. His origins were humble. He was born on 28 April 1937 at al-Ouja, a village near Takrit, a farming town on the Tigris 100 miles north of Baghdad. It was a poor community from which the peasants would ship their watermelons down river to the capital in animal-skin boats. He was born in a shack built of mud bricks, a fact of which he remained proud even after he developed imperial pretensions. He grew up in an impoverished society which was nominally Sunni but which was governed more by tribal and family customs than by the dictates of Islam. Sunnism is the majority orthodox doctrine of Islam, although in Iraq perhaps only one in five of Arabs is a Sunni. His father was said to have died before his birth, although the gossip which persisted even after his rise to power was that he was illegitimate. His mother, Subha Tulfah, remarried and, contrary to custom, Saddam was raised in the mud-brick house his mother shared with her new husband. Not only did the stepfather, Ibrahim al-Hassan, delight in beating the boy, but Saddam was also regarded as an outcast in the small peasant community because of his family situation. He carried a steel bar to protect himself from other boys as he made the daily trek to school in Takrit. If he could be said to have had a friend, it was his cousin, Adnan Khairallah, a future defence minister. Adnan's father, Khairallah Tulfah, who through Saddam was to become governor of Baghdad, virtually adopted him and, at the age of ten, his cousins gave him his first real possession – a revolver.

The atmosphere in which Saddam spent his youth was one of corruption, lawlessness and murder. The family were of lowly peasant background, but were feared as local brigands. This was a community in which casual violence and even murder enhanced the reputation of the perpetrator. In the place of any intellectual inspiration, Saddam had the prejudices of his uncle, a former soldier who in 1981 was to pen a Baathist tract entitled 'Three Whom God Should Not Have Created: Persians, Jews and Flies'. Khairallah Tulfah also provided Saddam with a wife – his daughter Sajida – and his first opportunity to kill, in this case a local rival with whom Khairallah had a feud. Saddam later related that his mother had told him at the age of four or five that Sajida had been betrothed to him by his grandfather. They became engaged while he was in Egypt and she in Iraq, and were married after the Baath came to power for the first time in 1963.

In later years Saddam's family prospered as his own power increased. Adnan and Khairallah Tulfah obtained high office and huge fortunes. But blood links were no guarantee of survival. It was said that when Saddam's relationship with a mistress, Samira, became too close, Adnan objected on behalf of his sister, Sajida. There was a family rift which only ended when Adnan was killed soon after in a suspicious helicopter crash.

The corrupt Khairallah Tulfah survived all the purges instituted by Saddam, but in the end his greed proved too much even for his nephew. Shortly before the Kuwait invasion, seventeen companies which he ran were wound up and their chief executives arrested.

By his late teens, Saddam was powerfully built and imposing, and already had a reputation as a murderer and a thug. In the late fifties he moved to Baghdad and settled in the run-down 'Tekarte' district, so called because it was where immigrants from Takrit congregated. He enrolled in law school although fellow students said he was rarely seen there, preferring to spend his time in the service

of his new-found cause – the Baath. The Baath was a tiny movement in Iraq which espoused the cause of a single pan-Arab state.
Saddam was twenty years old when he was recruited by Abdel-
Khalik Samarrai, a municipal clerk who was to become one of the
party's chief ideologues. Samarrai was to suffer a similar fate to
that of many who were close to Saddam in the early years: in 1973
he was arrested for alleged participation in a plot against Saddam,
by then vice-president, although the real reason was that Saddam
saw him as a rival. He was imprisoned in solitary confinement, the
worst punishment available since President Hassan al-Bakr refused
to authorize his execution. Then in 1979, when Saddam finally
pushed Bakr aside, Samarrai was taken out and shot.

Saddam's experience of killing stood him in good stead when he
joined the Baath Party in 1957. It was the year before the revolution
which overthrew the British-backed Hashemite monarchy and
brought to power Brigadier Abdel-Karim Qassem and his Free
Officers movement. The Baath supported the revolution and
initially co-operated with other opposition groups. But civilian
backing for Qassem's regime came principally from the much larger
Communist Party, and this engaged in an increasingly intense and
bloody fight for supremacy against its erstwhile allies, including the
pan-Arabist Baathists. Saddam's principal virtue, in the eyes of the
Baath, was as a willing enforcer and hit man in this ideological
struggle.

With the Communists in the ascendancy after Qassem took
control in 1958, the Baath leadership decided to assassinate President Qassem; a plan was devised and ready to implement by 1 June
1959. Ten men, including Saddam, were selected and trained to
participate in the hit squad, of whom eight were eventually chosen
to carry out the attack. For a while, however, the Baath leadership
gave the dictator the benefit of the doubt, encouraged by his moves
to distance himself from the excesses of the Communists. But on 14
July, the first anniversary of the revolution, the Communist Party
sent street fighters to the northern town of Kirkuk to wipe out its
pan-Arab opponents. The ensuing battle was in part a political
conflict, in part an ethnic clash between the city's Kurdish and

Turkoman communities. By official accounts, seventy-nine people were killed; forty of the victims were buried alive. Qassem dissociated himself from the violence but did little to restrain the Communists. The Baath decided it was time to act.

The plan was for the hit squad to corner Qassem's official car on its journey between his home and his office at the Defence Ministry. The location chosen was a narrow section of Rashid Street, a colonnaded thoroughfare between the north and south gates of Old Baghdad, where the plotters rented an apartment. One section of the hit squad was to block Qassem's route with a car, while the second group would rush from the apartment and open fire with machine guns.

The final decision to go ahead with the plan was taken on 1 October, though there were several false alarms before the alert came, on the evening of 7 October, that Qassem was on his way to Rashid Street, heading for a reception at the East German embassy.

The operation was a fiasco. Selim Zibaq, whose job was to move his car into the middle of the street to intercept Qassem, had mislaid his keys. While the gunmen were arguing about what to do next, Qassem's car arrived. One of the gunmen, Abdel-Wahab al-Ghariri, managed to open fire and kill the driver. But as he made for the car to kill Qassem he was shot dead by a bullet fired from across the street by one of his own comrades. In the confusion Saddam was shot in the leg and Samir Najm, another gunman, was hit in the chest. The survivors fled to a safe house and awaited confirmation that the dictator was dead, for they had seen him slump forward in the volley of bullets.

However, although Qassem had been wounded he was not dead and the army, which might have taken the opportunity to rise against him, remained loyal. The chief of staff, Salih Ahmad al-Abdi, announced to the nation that the Sole Leader had escaped the 'sinful hand' of the assassin with nothing worse than a slight shoulder wound.

With the passage of years and the rise of Saddam, the botched operation on Rashid Street was embroidered into a legend which underlined his qualities of daring, bravery and leadership. In officially sponsored accounts of the affair it is Saddam himself, then only twenty-two, who chose the location of the attack and rented the nearby apartment, and it was the wounded Saddam who covered the retreat of his comrades. In the relative safety of a Baath Party hideout, he is then said to have removed the bullet from his leg with a pair of scissors because, he claimed, a doctor was called but never arrived.

However, a doctor did arrive to treat the wounded. He was a Baathist student from the Baghdad College of Medicine named Tahsin Moallah. 'I was called to the safe house to treat two men who had been wounded,' Dr Moallah, an exile from Iraq since 1976, said in an interview with the authors. 'I first attended to Samir Najm, who had been hit in the chest, and cleaned his wounds. Then I saw a young man in the corner who had been hit in the shin. It was Saddam Hussein. It was the first time I had met him.'

Dr Moallah said Saddam's injury was superficial, 'like a knife wound'. 'I asked him what had happened to the bullet and he said he had taken it out himself.' And what of Saddam's claim that no doctor had arrived? 'If that is so,' said Dr Moallah, 'then why was I jailed for six months by the People's Court for providing medical attention to them?'

Of the seven survivors of the Qassem hit squad itself, some were caught and sentenced to death by the notoriously ruthless People's Court, presided over by Colonel Fadil Abbass al-Mahdawi. While Saddam and two others escaped together, some of the remaining assassins were rounded up on 23 October when police surrounded their hideout. They were among seventy-eight Baathists later tried in public by the Mahdawi court where their defiance and determination, despite having been tortured during interrogation, made a strong impression and heightened the Baath's status as a vanguard party of the masses. Few of the accused denied their role in the assassination plot and one of Saddam's fellow gunmen, Selim Zibaq, said he expected no mercy from a court which had become a farce. President Qassem postponed the death sentences against those most closely connected with the plot after being warned of a pan-Arabist uprising if they went ahead.

Of the two gunmen who remained at Saddam's side, Ahmad al-Azzuz was jailed after Saddam came to power, and Abdel-Karim al-Shaikhli went on to become foreign minister but was purged in 1971 and sent to the effective exile of the United Nations. Just after the start of the Gulf war, when Shaikhli was back in Baghdad, he drove with his wife to pay some bills. As he stepped from his car he was shot dead by two gunmen. No one intervened and the killers walked calmly away.

The doctor, Tahsin Moallah, almost certainly escaped a similar fate by fleeing the country in 1976. He was by then Dean of the College of Medicine and a senior member of the Baath Party, the Iraqi branch of which he had helped to found in the early 1950s. 'I would still call myself a Baathist. It is Saddam who has deviated,' he said of the man he came to know over a period of seventeen years.

I think the cause was lost in the early 1970s. There were many disagreements but one could only criticize up to a point. I left Baghdad on 3 April, 1976 and went to Kuwait. It was just a day before they issued an order that I shouldn't be allowed to leave the country. I worked in Kuwait at the Ministry of Health. On 20 June, 1977 I discovered a bomb under my car. It was so big that the expert who examined it, an American, said that if it had gone off, they wouldn't have been able to find a bone to bury. Saddam, you see, is afraid of anyone who might be able to reorganize the party. And, like the Communist Party under Stalin, the Baath has lost more people under Saddam's regime than under any other.

After the failed attack on Qassem's life, Saddam himself managed to escape to Syria and from there to Cairo. It was an episode which has been used to embellish the Saddam myth – a bedouin disguise, the perilous movement from hideout to hideout, the journey across the desert.

According to official history, Saddam fled to the home of his uncle and burned his personal photographs before heading north to Takrit. He is said to have disguised himself in bedouin robes and set off with only a knife for protection. He went on foot, despite his wound, following the course of the Tigris until he found a man who was willing to sell him his horse. He survived the journey on a diet of bread and dates and the occasional hospitality of the bedouin. Further details reinforce the image of his bravery and resourcefulness: how he argued his way out of a tight spot when stopped by customs men who thought he was a smuggler, how he swam across the Tigris, again despite his wound, with his knife clenched between his teeth. At al-Ouja he is said to have joined up with other Baathists to cross into Syria. They travelled at night, first by jeep and later by donkey, until they reached the border and crossed to Abu Kemal and from there to Deir al-Zor and finally to Damascus, where Saddam was to remain for the next six months.

Syria and Gamal-Abdel Nasser's Egypt at that time formed a unified country, the United Arab Republic, which had been formed in 1958, and in February 1960 Saddam moved from Damascus to Cairo. Ostensibly a student, his main activity for the next three years was to increase his stature in the Baath. He became a full member of the inner party, having up to then been only a probationer. The Egyptians tolerated the exiled Baathists, who formed a large community in Cairo, but it seems the intelligence services had reason to distrust Saddam, and they denied him the funding often disbursed to exiles. He nevertheless succeeded in getting a small retainer paid from the petty cash of the presidential palace. Saddam is said to have regarded life in Cairo as the equivalent of a prison sentence.

The three and a half years of exile until the Baathist-led coup which overthrew Qassem in 1963 are the most obscure of Saddam's often shadowy and contradictory history. The failed assassination attempt in 1959 in which Saddam played his part had created a rift in Baathist ranks, because a small group of the party's regional (Iraqi) leadership had gone ahead with the attempt without the direct approval of the national (pan-Arab) leadership, then based in Damascus. After the failure of the plot some Baath leaders abandoned the party believing that it should not resort to criminal acts. However, the organizer of the plot, Fuad al-Rikabi, justified the assassination attempt on the grounds that Qassem was a traitor to pan-Arabism and that the attack had the approval of the masses. As a result of the split, the Iraqi party in exile was dissolved and reformed under a new leadership. Ali Saleh Saadi, who was to become deputy premier after the 1963 coup, was appointed secretary of the new Iraqi party in 1962 and made clear his opposition to those responsible for the botched murder attempt.

It was Saadi's party that finally took control of Iraq with a bloody coup on 8 February 1963 that overturned the Qassem regime. This so-called Ramadan Revolution was mounted by a group of Baathist army officers, although the Baath disguised its role, preferring to hide behind the anonymity of a National Council for the Revolutionary Command.

At the behest of Ali Saleh Saadi, the secretary of the Baath, Abdel Salem Aref was installed as provisional president – Aref was one of the leaders, with Qassem, of the 1958 revolution but had subsequently been purged by the dictator, tried and sentenced to death. In line with his usual practice, Qassem had left the sentence unsigned and Aref lived to join the plot against him. Aref felt no such scruples and had Qassem executed the day after the coup. Perhaps it was from this that the young Saddam learnt the lesson that, once in power, it was safer to liquidate one's opponents rather than leave them to fight another day.

Saddam had returned to Iraq after the coup, to find the party still riven by ideological struggle. Between the right and the left factions (the latter led by Saadi), a centrist faction held sway, led by Saddam's relative, the former army officer from Takrit, Hassan al-Bakr. Saddam was soon seen, gun in hand, acting as bodyguard for Bakr.

The leftists wanted to give priority to the introduction of socialism, and warned against relying on the military elements who had organized the Ramadan Revolution. But Saadi, the deputy premier in the new regime, was criticized as trying to impose single party rule, rather than co-operating with other nationalist groups. In an effort to reconcile the factions, Michel Aflaq, the Syrian founder of Baath, was brought to Baghdad. But he effectively supported the rightist group.

Saddam, sensing that the opponents of Saadi were in the ascendancy, also allied himself with the rightists and the moderates and openly criticized the deputy premier. It was a clever strategy and resulted in his election to the general council of the Baath's regional (Iraqi) command. This apparent moderation, however, did not diminish his predilection for violent solutions: he went to Talib Shabib, the foreign minister and leader of the rightist faction with an offer to assassinate Saadi. Shabib turned it down on the grounds, he later told his party comrades, that if Saddam were allowed to go ahead he feared he might be the next victim.

Aflaq now directed that the leftists, including Saadi, should be expelled from the party and sent into exile. But this led to street demonstrations on behalf of Saadi's group and only exacerbated the tensions. On 18 November, just nine months after the February coup the military decided to restore order. President Aref ordered the arrest of both the national and regional Commands, including Aflaq, who was to become Saddam's chief mentor and promoter. He was kept under arrest for a day before being sent back to Damascus.

The factionalism within the Baath and the relative inexperience of members of what had been an underground organization led to the downfall of the Baathist government. The army, exasperated by the ineptitude of their civilian partners and disgusted by the excesses of the Baath militia, believed they had to step in to take direct control. It would be five years before the Baath again achieved power in Iraq.

Following the coup, the Baathist militia, the National Guard, the main function of which had been to suppress the Communists and other opponents, was dissolved. Bakr, who had been prime minister in the Baathist government, survived until the following year as vice-president but gradually he and other Baathists were removed from positions of power. The remnants of the discredited Baath turned to clandestine operations, working through on a paramilitary network of cells. In this situation Saddam's talents for violence and intrigue served him well. The officially-sponsored accounts relate how he organized his comrades, purchased weapons and obtained explosives for bomb attacks, and how he always travelled with a machine gun and a revolver at the ready.

It was small wonder then that in 1964, five years after his participation in the attempt on the life of Qassem, he was chosen to assassinate the head of state, Aref. Once again the plot failed, this time because an officer who was crucial to the plan had been transferred and the attack had to be aborted. The officer would have let Saddam and a small hit team into a conference room where Aref and the military National Revolutionary Council was meeting so they could machine gun them to death.

While Saddam's re-emergence as an assassin was no surprise, his meteoric rise to power within the re-formed Baath Party was remarkable. He is said to have travelled to Syria to persuade Aflaq, the founder of the Baath and leader of the national command, to dissolve the leadership of the Iraqi branch. Aflaq not only concurred, but appointed Saddam secretary – and therefore head – of a caretaker leadership in February 1964. Such an appointment was unprecedented, in that Saddam had held no junior leadership role within the Baath. In the eyes of some contemporary Baath activists the appointment defied logic. Those who subsequently turned against Saddam conjectured that Aflaq was persuaded by some unnamed external power to place Saddam in command. A more likely explanation is that Aflaq felt the party in Iraq needed to be rebuilt along paramilitary lines by a civilian party loyalist who would keep the Baathist army officers under control. Saddam appeared to be his ideal man.

However, the arrangement whereby Saddam was sole leader of the Iraqi party lasted for no more than three months, after which Abdel-Karim al-Shaikhli was appointed co-leader. Shaikhli, who Saddam was used to calling 'my twin brother' – at least until he was purged in 1971 – was gunned down in a Baghdad street shortly after the outbreak of the Gulf war.

After the aborted assassination plot against Aref, the Baath leadership plotted a coup d'état in September 1964. Their plans were uncovered by the police and there was a wave of arrests. Saddam's opponents claim that after he was arrested he handed over details of the Baath structure to the authorities. Certainly, while in jail he was spared the torture routinely inflicted on his comrades. Taher Yahya, the prime minister, gave the order that he was not to be harmed, a dispensation which could also be explained by the fact that Taher Yahya, too, was from Takrit.

During the brief Baathist ascendancy in 1963, Saddam had been attached to the Baath's paramilitary National Guard; after 1963, he led the underground Jihaz Hunain, an elite hit squad and intelligence unit at the heart of the Baath party which he used as a power base to dominate party affairs. Just as the party had no programme for coming to power through the ballot box, so Saddam had no intention of allowing democratic decisions to determine the direction of the party.

By 1964, at the age of twenty-seven, he was the full-time organizer of the civilian wing of the party. He had close allies in Bakr, Hardan Takriti and Salih Mahdi Ammash, all of whom came from Takrit – Bakr, of course, he later deposed, Ammash he exiled and Hardan Takriti he had murdered in Kuwait. In 1966 Saddam seized the post of deputy secretary general of the party at gunpoint and began the process of building an inner circle of intimates, usually his relatives, on whom he would base his absolute rule.

So far as he was known to the Iraqi people at this stage, it was as a thug and a gunman, part of the gang who tried to kill Qassem. In the standard work on republican Iraq by the Iraq academic Majid Khadduri, published in 1969, 'Sudam Takriti' rates only one mention and a footnote, both relating to the abortive attempt on Qassem's life. Veterans of the period, both among those who opposed him at the time or who fell foul of him later, invariably dwell on his lowly origins, his lack of culture, and his apparent lack of moral values. Perhaps it was in reaction to this that Saddam felt it necessary to reinvent himself and to seek legitimacy through fanciful claims to a more illustrious descent. But this was only after he had achieved total power.

On 17 July 1968 a group made up of senior officers and members of the Baath including Saddam seized power in Baghdad in a bloodless coup; but it was a regime which could not last, for the

Baath always intended to exercise total control, so on 30 July came a second revolution, which ensured that the Baath held all the levers of power. Bakr was made president, and Saddam Hussein, the civilian, was made deputy to this last surviving member of the Free Officers who carried out the bloody revolution of 14 July 1958 which had overthrown the monarchy.

One of the plotters in 1968 was Abdul Razzaq al-Nayef, the military intelligence chief of the government then in power. Nayef was not a Baathist but decided to throw in his lot with the conspirators in exchange for a promise of high office, and immediately after the 17 July coup, Nayef was named prime minister. Before the coup, however, in which Saddam led the tank assault on the presidential palace, he had already resolved to eliminate Nayef and had received the party's approval for the assassination. Nayef was useful only because he could bring military backing for the Baathist coup. In the event, Saddam decided to send Nayef into exile as ambassador to Morocco; this was evidence of the weakness of the Baathist position in the early days, rather than a gesture of mercy on Saddam's part. He personally escorted Nayef to the military airport, all the while with a pistol in his pocket aimed at the erstwhile prime minister. There was a familiar postscript to Nayef's career: in July 1978, a squad of the Estikhbarat – military intelligence agents responsible for overseas operations – shot him dead on the steps of a London hotel.

It was not long before Saddam became known as the power behind the throne of President Bakr. Although he had yet to develop the personality cult which later became so overpowering, with its kitsch version of Iraq's imperial past, it was soon apparent that he liked to construct historical endorsements for his policies.

In the early 1970s he had ordered the rebuilding of Babylon, and, even before the war with Iran, he was comparing himself with Nebuchadnezzar, the king who held the children of Israel captive 'by the waters of Babylon' in the sixth century BC.

Nebuchadnezzar stirs in me everything relating to pre-Islamic ancient history [he said in 1979]. I am reminded that any human being with broad horizons, faith and feeling can act wisely but practically, attain his goals and become a great man who makes his country into a great state. And what is most important to me about Nebuchadnezzar is the link between the Arabs' abilities and the liberation of Palestine. Nebuchadnezzar was, after all, an Arab from Iraq, albeit ancient Iraq. Nebuchadnezzar was the one who brought the bound Jewish slaves from Palestine. That is why I like to remind the Arabs, Iraqis in particular, of their historical responsibilities. It is a burden that should not stop them from action, but rather spur them into action because of their history.

But it was not until after the start of the Gulf war in 1980 that Saddam launched his personality cult in earnest. It's aim, at this stage, to portray him as a military leader, for the practical reason that he did not want the real generals to take the credit for what at the time seemed to be a successful assault on Iran. Saddam himself, despite his uniforms, titles and honorific ranks, had never had any military experience, had probably never read a military textbook or ever considered the finer points of strategy or tactics, and had never taken part in armed conflict.

Now he suddenly became the commander-in-chief, a field marshal directing his armies. It was one of the few propaganda mistakes he made, for so effectively was the myth of Saddam the war leader propagated that he became personally identified with the conflict. When things were going well, that was fine, but that was a very brief period: only for the first two years of the Gulf war were the Iraqi troops able to maintain the tenuous foothold they had established on Iranian soil. For the next six years they grimly defended their own borders, and, although they did that very well, it could hardly be construed as a victory.

So Saddam's campaign to build himself up as a war leader rebounded, and it was only after Iran was forced to the conference table that he could once again emerge as the military man. Gradually, the huge posters of Saddam in uniform were brought back, to complement all the others showing him in Kurdish dress, or wearing the keffiyeh of the Arabs of the south, the business suit of the diplomat, or the casual wear of the rich, Westernized elite.

With the end of the war came an even more remarkable transformation: no longer was Saddam content to be portrayed as merely the first Iraqi, a man like other men except that he was superior to them, more powerful, stronger, cleverer. Now came the illusion of grandeur, the effort to show Saddam as the inheritor of the glories of the great kingdoms of the past which occupied the land of modern Iraq. At the celebrations of his birthday in his hometown of Takrit in 1990, Saddam allowed himself to be identified with Sargon the Great, the ruler of the Empire of Agade, the first great state to arise in the land between the two rivers. There were tableaux showing the legend of Sargon's birth – like Moses, found floating in a rush basket among the reeds of a river – and the great battles he went on to fight and win. Sargon was reputed to have triumphed in battle thirty-four times, decimating his foes as he expanded his empire from the Lower Sea – the Gulf – to the Middle Sea – the Mediterranean.

The Empire of Agade flourished around 2300 BC, and though the legend of the great ruler is still taught to Iraqi children, it was later kings who became the models for the newly ennobled Saddam. Hammurabi, the great law-giver of the eighteenth century BC, who was famed for protecting the weak from the strong and the poor from the rich, whose stele setting out just and far-reaching laws can still be seen in the Baghdad museum, became the first of the new role models.

Posters all over Iraq showed Saddam receiving the heritage of Babylon from Hammurabi, its founder, and the quickly revised text books reminded people that Hammurabi was not only a law-giver but a fighting soldier who reduced the cities of his enemies to dust.

At Babylon, Saddam had built a vast reproduction of the ancient city, once the capital of an area stretching from Kuwait in the south to Israel in the north, taking in what is now Jordan, Syria and Lebanon. Defying good archaeological practice, Saddam decreed that reproductions of the ancient buildings of Babylon should be built on the original sites, so millions of special bricks were made, each one stamped with the tugra or mark of Saddam Hussein, just as Nebuchadnezzar had his imprint on many of the original building blocks. After the invasion of Kuwait sanctions stopped the work, and the restaurants around the vast artificial lake were closed, but still the posters and the souvenirs were on sale, and in every booklet detailing Nebuchadnezzar's great rule, his feats in thrice conquering Jerusalem and taking the Israelites into captivity, the stern face of Saddam Hussein the military leader stares out.

Every Iraqi understood the message, but one of the archaeologists working at the site spelled it out. 'Babylon was built in ancient times, and was a great city, so now it must be built into a great city again in the time of our new great leader, Saddam Hussein,' said Shafqa Mohammed Jaafar.

Saddam, the anti-imperialist revolutionary, also presided over a quasi-royalist revival. The cemetery of the Hashemite kings was refurbished and there he would take distinguished guests such as King Hussein of Jordan. Saddam began to style himself al-Hashemi, the Hashemite, and to refer to King Hussein as his cousin. The official rumour mill put about the story that he was, in fact, the son of the late King Ghazi, the product of a secret but legitimate liaison between the monarch and Saddam's mother Subha Tulfa. Throughout the country, he had eighty-three palaces at his personal disposal.

There were even signs that Saddam had come to believe his own propaganda. In a remarkable letter to the Egyptian president, Hosni Mubarak, three weeks after the invasion of Kuwait, Saddam referred to himself thus:

The speaker himself was the son of a farmer whose father died months before his birth. He came from a noble family whose prime honour lay in its work, and in that it descended from the Kuraishi Mohamedan family to which the Imam al-Hussein, our forefather, the son of Imam Ali bin abi Talib belonged. To my knowledge, Your Excellency, you are from an Egyptian family that is not related to princes or kings . . .

Saddam, therefore, was a descendant of the prophet while Mubarak was merely a commoner.

This cult of personality, the personification of the state in the person of one man, went on in Baghdad even as the Kuwait invasion drew closer. A twelve-feet high bronze statue of Saddam was erected in September 1990, to join the huge models of his hands holding scimitars which form triumphal arches in the capital, arches leading to the buildings he decreed – the strange new tomb of the unknown soldier built like twin shields rising from the ground, the vast ministries, the palace for himself which employed twenty-five Portuguese and two Belgians purely to work on the marble which was to line its halls.

Radio and television broadcasts were dominated by a constant recital of his activities, daily repetitions of his past feats and an evergrowing stream of his official and honorific titles: president, commander-in-chief, leader of the national command, hero of Qaddissiyeh, knight of the Arab nation, al-faris al-mighwar – the daring and aggressive knight.

Yet in the run-up to the Western move to expel Iraq from Kuwait, the dictator who was seen so regularly on Iraqi television during the Gulf war was strangely absent. For weeks he would not even appear on television in case the agents of America could identify where he was and lay on an instant air strike, or fire rockets at the studios. In those first weeks Saddam became paranoid about his own personal safety, and ascribed huge powers of detection and destruction to the Americans.

Diplomats and the curious procession of former politicians who beat a path to Saddam's door to win restored glory by persuading him to release some hostages were kept waiting for hours, then taken by circuitous routes to little-used offices for their meeting with the great man, usually after dark. Yasser Arafat, well aware of the need for security after his thirty years of struggle, plotting and intrigue, was kept fuming for almost twelve hours before his midnight meeting with Saddam, a taste of the ordeal to which he regularly subjected his own callers.

Nowhere were Saddam's dynastic pretensions more apparent than in his treatment of his family and close circle. By the end of the Gulf war virtually all key posts were held by a few hundred individuals from his clan in Takrit and the town itself had changed from an impoverished backwater into a provincial metropolis. In each institution, in the party, the army, the government and the secret police, there was always a loyal Takriti; nominal authority might belong to an outsider but the real power always rested with a member of the inner circle.

Political alliances were cemented by ties of marriage which bound the most prominent members of the regime to Saddam and him to them. There was one law for the family and one for the rest, so that when his eldest son, Uday, killed Saddam's Christian bodyguard in a drunken brawl in 1988, the young man's punishment was temporary exile. Saddam announced that Uday must go on trial and pay for his crime but he bowed to the 'insistent demands' of the victim's family that he should show mercy.

Clan politics played a significant part in controlling the institutions of state, and despite his undoubted abilities as a modern leader Saddam had an atavistic attachment to some of the old tribal ways. According to an Arab journalist who met him on several occasions: 'At one moment, Saddam could put his mind to the complexities of the transfer of high technology while at the next he would be involved in sorting out some obscure argument over a clan marriage.'

While Saddam often showed himself capable of extreme brutality, he could be a man of some charm and charisma. During the Gulf war he personally led the drive to persuade people to support Iraq's dwindling reserves by handing over their valuables. Night after night on television there were scenes of well-dressed ladies calling at the palace to hand over their rings and necklaces, jewels and family heirlooms. Of course, it was partly the result of pressure, of a feeling that there would be a black mark, at least, against a rich family that did not take part. But it was also plain from the conversation of the society ladies of Baghdad that the chance of meeting the leader, of being seen with him on television, played its part in persuading them to this extreme of patriotism.

One of the present authors had a personal example of Saddam's charm many years earlier. During a rather boring dinner given by the Ministry of Information in honour of a visiting delegation, Saddam, then vice-president, unexpectedly turned up, and was quickly given the seat of honour in the middle of the centre table. Looking around, he spotted the one obvious Westerner present, and soon a message was brought over to say the vice-president would like the stranger to join him. A place was laid, and in the Iraqi way, a bottle of Black Label Scotch was placed strategically between the guest and Saddam. The agreeable dinner was served in the open-air on this balmy spring evening, and attentive waiters made sure the glasses of Scotch were never empty: as the dinner ended, so did the bottle of Scotch. Both vice-president and guest walked steadily away. Neither, it was clear, were strangers to alcohol.

Nor is Saddam without a sense of humour: at that same dinner he recalled through an interpreter that the only previous Ministry of Information dinner he had attended had been in honour of a troupe of visiting North Korean dancers. At the end of their visit, he said, the North Koreans warmly invited an Iraqi cultural group to go to Pyongyang 'That was almost a year ago, and we still haven't been able to find anyone who will go.'

A rougher side of Saddam's character was shown during another visit we paid to Baghdad, again during his time as vice-president. It was a period of unrest, with riots in the Shia cities of Kerbala and Najjaf being brutally suppressed by the police and paramilitary forces. Then one day came news of trouble much closer to home, in a newly built working-class area of Baghdad itself named after Saddam. Word of the violence reached the palace as Saddam was going into a meeting. Flying into a rage, he ran to his car and jumped into the driving seat. Without waiting for his bodyguards he took off at high speed for the trouble spot. Once there he pulled up outside the central mosque where crowds had gathered as shops were broken into, stalls overturned and makeshift barricades put up in the streets.

Shouldering his way through the crowd he strode up to the top step and turned to face the surprised audience, who quickly recognized the distinctive jowly features. 'What do you think you're doing,' he shouted. 'What good will this do you, destroying your own property, your own place. You damn fools, stand still and listen to me . . .'

As his flustered convoy of bodyguards arrived minutes later, he gestured them away as he began a dialogue with the crowd, who by now were laughing and shouting their approval of the vice-president's effrontery. Iraqis love a tough guy, a ruler who knows what he wants and has no fear of his own people. Saddam scores well on both counts.

This is at least one of the clues to how such a man came to rule Iraq and to turn it into the biggest military power in the Middle East.

The Creation of the Baathist State

On 24 June 1989 Saddam Hussein drove in convoy to Saddam International Airport with senior officials of party and state to receive the mortal remains of Michel Aflaq and to help carry his coffin from the plane which had flown it from France.

For one who had been so intimately connected with the internecine politics of Iraq for almost four decades, the seventy-nine-year-old founder of the Baath party had the rare privilege of dying in his bed, or rather in a hospital bed in Paris where he had undergone unsuccessful heart surgery.

Saddam Hussein's rise to power was through the Baath Party, the political organization which under his leadership came to permeate every stratum of Iraqi life. Membership of the party, once the privilege of an activist elite, was expanded into a mass movement in the 1970s; but the early doctrine of 'inner party' and 'outer party' remained, with the selected cadres wielding power far beyond their nominal titles or positions. It was they who controlled the security apparatus which became the true guarantor of the stability of the regime; political commissars from the party were seconded to every military formation from battalion level upwards, and had the authority in certain circumstances to countermand the instructions of the military commanders.

Party members were at the heart of the intelligence agencies, watching over every citizen, every organization, and every ministry of the state. By ensuring that these party members were directly identified with the results of the decisions they made – forcing them to take part in arrests, brutal interrogations and even executions – Saddam ensured their complicity in the excesses of the regime.

The Baath was a pan-Arabist movement which in the forty years since its foundation in 1949 gained political power only in Syria and in Iraq. In Syria, the Baath appealed to the politically aware, and to the nationalist feelings of Syrians, but in Iraq, there was nothing intellectual about the party, no well-defined programme, no reliance on the appeal of the policies being put forward. Rather, the party consisted of quite separate cells pursuing local goals: they might band together for some national objective, though there was never any certainty of that; only if the group leaders saw personal advantage in going along with the activities of another branch of the party would there be concerted action. This was not so much a political party, more an umbrella organization for bands of thugs, strong-arm men and murderers, all of whom were hoping to seize power by force, and plotting against each other as much as against the government of the day.

Two years before the second Baathist coup of 1968, Michel Aflaq's party old guard was bloodily ousted from Syria by the military wing of the party. He sought refuge in Baghdad, where he was given the title of secretary-general of the national command, the supposedly pan-Arab leadership of the party. In 1971 in Damascus he was sentenced to death in absentia for treason against his native Syria.

Aflaq's presence lent legitimacy to Saddam's rule, although the older man had lost all political power long before his acolyte took over the presidency of Iraq. Aflaq nevertheless served as a figure-head for the regime's declared pan-Arabist ideals and as a last link with earlier struggles in the 1940s and 1950s. His presence also legitimized the split between Iraq and Syria, with both regimes claiming to uphold the sacred flame of Baathism.

Salah al-Din Bitar, co-founder of Baathism with Aflaq, was a more practical man, who had experience of ministerial office in Damascus, and a clearer viewpoint; he saw that far from attempting to further the Baathist philosophy of pan-Arabism, the President of Syria, Hafez al-Assad, was becoming more and more cut off from the mass of the people, and was ruling through his own Alawi group, just as Saddam Hussein relied more and more on the Takriti clique. Bitar tried to argue in favour of constitutional freedom and a broader base for the party; it was hopeless, as he had the sense to see, fleeing into exile in Paris where he founded a newspaper highly critical of both the Iraqi and the Syrian regimes. He was gunned down just off the Champs Elysée on 21 July 1980, shot once in the back of the head by a professional assassin who used a silenced pistol. No one ever doubted that it was the Iraqis who pulled the trigger, taking vengeance against one of the founders of their party who spoke out against the excesses of the regime, and who refused to join his friend and colleague Aflaq in Baghdad and support that section of the divided party.

Michel Aflaq was born into a lower middle class Greek Orthodox family in Damascus in 1910, when Syria, Iraq, Palestine and Arabia were part of the Ottoman empire. Aflaq's father, although an active opponent of French colonial rule, sent his son to the Sorbonne where he studied from 1928–32 and where he was exposed to the intellectual currents of Europe between the wars; he returned from Europe fired by the same ideologies which inspired Hitler and the National Socialists.

His time in Paris also allowed him to experience at first hand how far the once barbarous West had overtaken the Arab world in terms of progress and enlightenment. Aflaq evolved his own philosophy based on a romantic synthesis of socialism, anti-colonialism and nostalgia for the past glories of the Arab world, coupled with admiration for the secular modernism of the West. Only by breaking down the colonial borders, eradicating backwardness and ignorance and reuniting the divided nation, Aflaq believed, could the Arabs be restored to their former glory. Although he was born a Christian and was politically a secularist, Aflaq later taught that Islam was the greatest cultural expression of the Arabs. Most Arab nationalists opposed the concept of Islam as a political force.

The Turks, who emerged as the dominant military power in the region in the Middle Ages, had justified their conquests in the name of Islam and imposed their despotic rule by recourse to Islamic sharia law. The Ottoman sultan held the title of caliph of the Muslims and official historians lent added authority to the caliphate by producing spurious genealogies for the sultans which purported to show their Arab origin and their direct descent from the tribe of the Prophet Mohammed. After he took over the presidency of Iraq in 1979, Saddam Hussein followed this example and had a family tree produced which was intended to prove his descent from both the Prophet and from Ali, the fourth Caliph of the Muslims and the founder of Shiism.

At its foundation Baathism was a secular doctrine. Unlike the Arab Communists, who believed in an international socialism which would span racial and geographical divides, the Baathists dreamt of recreating the Arab state which once stretched across North Africa, the Levant, and Arabia and as far as the foothills of Iran. It was a doctrine inspired by the depths to which the Arab nation had sunk in 400 years of Ottoman rule and by the conspiracies of the European powers to keep the Arabs in a state of neo-colonialist subjugation.

The Baathist movement which Aflaq formed in the early 1940s was an inspiration, above all, to the impoverished and alienated lower middle class. The founders of the Baath shared the Nazis' nostalgia for a mythical and glorious past and their quasi-mystical desire for the reunification of a nation which had been divided and dispossessed by the machinations of outside powers. Like Nazism in Europe, Baathism became in the Middle East both the reflection and antithesis of Marxism. The establishment of socialism was among its slogans, but the unity of the Arab nation came first. It also shared with European fascism a belief in strong leadership and in the expediency of political violence. The pillars of the party would be highly moral, highly disciplined youths whose ideals would carry the people with them; there was never an intention to gain power through the ballot box. The 'Amid' or doyen of the party was to be its unquestioned leader and guide who would preside over a pyramidal power structure. Aflaq – bookish, physically timid and a poor organizer – was ill suited to this charismatic role; he found in Saddam Hussein his ideal of the brave, ruthless and dedicated Arab hero.

Aflaq taught that the Arabs should never lose their sense of nationalism or 'confuse it with the felonious notion of class interests'. This was a doctrine which brought the Baath into an obvious conflict with Communism; the programme of the Baath issued in July 1943 began with the statement: 'We represent the Arab spirit against materialist Communism.' The Marxist theoretician, Yasin al-Hafiz, wrote retrospectively of the foundation of Baathism that 'at a time when the Arab national movement became the expression of the aspirations of emancipation of a divided and oppressed people, the Arab nationalist petty bourgeoisie suddenly began to speak in German. German and Italian nationalist terms became part of the vocabulary of the Arab nationalist petty bourgeoisie'.

In the struggle for power in Iraq, Baathists and Communists would occasionally make common cause – the Communists for example gave the Baathists their first printing press – but there always remained between them a deep ideological divide. Once in power, Saddam Hussein adopted a neo-Marxist rhetoric of revolution and anti-imperialism which gave the false impression that Iraq had fallen into the Soviet camp, particularly after the two countries signed a friendship and co-operation agreement in 1972. But the relationship was never more than an alliance of convenience, even though early Baathist tracts were censored or rewritten to show that the party had always been first and foremost socialist, progressive and democratically organized.

Throughout the 1960s, in fact, Baathism was recognized by the West as a useful counterweight to the spread of Communism in the region. Western hegemony in the Arab states on the Soviet Union's southern flank was crumbling under pressure from Nasserism in Egypt, a civil war in Lebanon, and by the 1958 coup which brought Brigadier Qassem to power in Iraq with the backing of the Communist party. US forces landed troops in Lebanon to prevent the nationalist upsurge spreading and also to threaten the new Iraqi regime with intervention if it tampered with Western oil interests. A motive for the suspicion with which Saddam and other Baathist exiles were later treated by Nasser's secret police was that they were suspected of having dealings with the CIA; Saddam himself was said to have made regular visits to the US embassy when he was in exile in Cairo.

After Qassem was overthrown by the Baathist military coup of 8 February 1963, the Paris magazine *L'Express* wrote: 'The Iraqi coup was inspired by the CIA. The British government and Nasser himself were aware of the putsch preparations.' Qassem had revealed just four days before the coup that he had received a warning from the US State Department that America would impose sanctions against Iraq if it went ahead with plans to exploit untapped oil concessions recovered from the foreign multinationals in 1961. The Baathist coup of 1963 headed off this threat to Western interests but it also provoked one of the bloodiest periods of Iraq's violent history.

Ali Saleh Saadi, the left-wing Baathist whom Saddam was to help oust from the party leadership later that year had been put in charge of plotting the coup in co-ordination with sympathizers in the military, led by Saddam's distant cousin from Takrit, Ahmed Hassan al-Bakr. On the day of the coup, Baathist officers led the military assault on Qassem's headquarters and other key installations and the Communists responded by calling on the masses to take to the streets. 'Destroy the treacherous conspirators and imperialist agents without mercy,' they said in a proclamation to their followers. There followed three days of murderous clashes; leftist and Baathist gangs gunned each other down in the streets until Qassem was executed and his bullet-ridden body was displayed on television: that ended the Communist resistance.

In the following weeks before they were thrown out in November, Baathist thugs wearing the uniform of the National Guard hunted down hundreds of leftists, using names and addresses provided by the CIA, then tortured and summarily executed them, despite their assurances to the Americans that members of the Communist party would be put on trial before courts martial.

After the Baathists the military, under Abdel-Salaam Aref and later under his brother Abdel-Rahman Aref, presided for five years over a series of civilian–military governments which promoted a Nasserite version of Arab nationalism. The Baath, whose image had suffered from the excesses of 1963, retreated into a period of reorganization and recruitment, the latter masterminded by Saddam Hussein. But after five years in power, the Nasserites had been undermined by economic problems, a civil war in Kurdistan and general social malaise. Military regimes in Iraq and elsewhere in the Middle East also faced public obloquy for the Arab defeat at the hands of Israel in 1967, with the loss of Jerusalem and the West Bank.

In Iraq, the right-wing of the Baath party, led by Saddam and Bakr, was in the ascendancy, and by early 1968, it was clear that the party was poised to take power. Nasser even sent a warning to the Iraqi prime minister, Taher Yahya, that Egyptian intelligence had learnt of a Baathist plot to stage a coup 'for the benefit of the CIA'. 'In every ministry,' said a former official, 'there would be one or two people known to be Baathists. With the future in mind, everyone would try to favour them.' When the coup came in July 1968, there were many who speculated that the Baath would not last long and that the military would reassert itself. They were not to know that the era of Saddam Hussein had dawned. Nor that, in the end, the sorely battered ideals of the Baath would take second place to the personal aspirations of Saddam.

The most important thing that Aflaq taught the future dictator was a sense of Arab history; Saddam had a passion for the past and references to the former glories of the Arab world peppered his speeches. But the lesson he learnt from Iraqi history was that the country was ungovernable except through repression and fear, and occasional generosity from above. Rule had to be 'with an iron fist and an open hand'. To survive against internal enemies and foreign conspiracies, one had to be ruthless.

As a boy, Aflaq had witnessed the departure of the Ottomans, followed by a brief interlude of chaotic freedom under the Syrian National Congress and, by 1920, the institution of French colonial rule.

The empire of the Turks was destroyed in the First World War by the great powers of the day, Britain and France. But, in order to gain allies in the fight, the British and the French had made promises which they later broke. As early as 1915, the British government assured Hussein, the Hashemite sherif of Mecca, that Britain would recognize and support the independence of the Arabs once the war was over. Believing that sovereignty over Syria and Palestine would go to Sherif Hussein and his followers once the Turks were defeated, the peninsula Arabs revolted against their Ottoman masters under the active guidance of British officers such as Colonel T. E. Lawrence.

In secret, however, France and Britain reached an understanding on Asia Minor, the so-called Sykes–Picot agreement of 1916 under which the post-Ottoman Middle East would be divided into French and British areas of influence.

In the same year, a new wartime government in Britain, headed by David Lloyd George and with Arthur Balfour as foreign secretary, had begun to look more kindly on the emerging Zionist movement that sought the establishment of a national home for the Jews. This change was partly an expression of realpolitik: Zionist ideas had already taken a strong hold on Jewish opinion in the United States and the British government hoped to gain the support of influential American Jews in its efforts to persuade the United States to join the allied war effort against Germany and Turkey. The policy led, in November 1917, to the Balfour Declaration in which the foreign secretary announced that the British government 'viewed with favour the establishment in Palestine of a national home for the Jewish people'. Almost as an afterthought and perhaps to placate those in Britain who had pointed out that Palestine was already populated, the declaration added that 'nothing shall be done which may prejudice the civil and religious rights of existing non-Jewish communities in Palestine'. The following month British forces conquered Palestine and entered Jerusalem.

When the war ended, both Arabs and Jews believed themselves to be the rightful heirs of post-Ottoman Palestine. The Arabs expected that their role in defeating the Turks would now make them masters of their own destiny in an independent Middle East. But the French and British had already made their own arrangements for carving up Syria and the Levant between them.

The Arabs came to regard the Sykes–Picot agreement and the Balfour Declaration as the twin pillars of a grand conspiracy, involving the European powers and world Zionism, to divide and colonize the Arab world and maintain its people in a state of subjugation. This perception of Western treachery and betrayal inspired the growth of pan-Arabism and continued, late into the twentieth century, to form the world view of Arab leaders such as Saddam Hussein.

Under Sykes–Picot, Britain and France were to have ruled Palestine as a condominium but the British government was determined to establish exclusive control over a territory which commanded the approach to the Suez Canal and the passage to India. The entry of Lord Allenby's forces into Jerusalem not only sealed the defeat of the Turks, but also ensured British dominance of Palestine in the post-war settlement. The British conquest led to a revision of the Sykes–Picot agreement by which the British would get Palestine and Mesopotamia (Iraq) and the French would get Syria. To appease the democratic sensibilities of the wartime ally, the United States, and its president, Woodrow Wilson, this colonialist division of the spoils of war was given an emancipatory gloss in an Anglo–French joint declaration, issued after the 1918 armistice, which said that the object of the war in the Middle East had been 'the complete and final liberation of the peoples who have for so long been oppressed by the Turks'.

But far from achieving their independence, the Arabs became the subjects of new masters, albeit under the terms of League of Nations mandates which were intended to foster the emergence of independent local administrations. In reality, however, the European powers treated their new acquisitions in much the same way that they treated their colonies. As Jawaharlal Nehru noted, League of Nations mandates were the equivalent of 'appointing a tiger to look after the interests of a number of cows or deer'.

In Syria, France dismissed the newly-formed Arab administration, instituted direct rule and carved away parts of Syria to enlarge the province of its Maronite allies in Mount Lebanon, ceding other territories to the new state of Turkey.

Under the Ottomans, Syria had been relatively outward-looking. It had been subjected to European influence from the nineteenth century, and the first stirrings of Arab nationalism pre-dated the First World War. Aflaq's father had been among those jailed by the Turks for nationalist agitation.

Iraq, by contrast, was a tribal backwater, ignorant and impoverished even by the standards of the decaying Ottoman Empire. In 1914, at the outbreak of war, troops from British India landed at the Shatt al-Arab and moved north to take the port of Basra. It took a bloody two-and-a-half year campaign for the British expeditionary forces to reach Baghdad and it was only after the armistice that they succeeded in taking the northern oil city of Mosul.

What emerged as Iraq after the First World War was, in many ways, the least Arab of Arab countries. It was cut off from its Arab neighbours in the west and south by the great deserts; it was bordered in the north by Turks, in the east by Persians. Its population included Kurds, Chaldeans, Assyrians and Turkomans. Even among its Moslems, allegiance was split between the Sunnis and the Shias. It was an unpromising soil in which to plant the doctrines of pan-Arabism; yet Baghdad had once been the cultural centre of the Arab world under the Abbasid caliph, Harun al-Rashid, before it fell to the Mongols, the Turkomans, the Persians, and finally the Ottomans.

Under the Ottomans, the territory which was to become Iraq formed three separate governates – that of Basra in the south, Baghdad in the centre and Mosul in the north. The Arab-populated governates of Basra and Baghdad, which straddled the valley of the Tigris and the Euphrates, were known collectively as Mesopotamia. Mosul province was a distinct entity, peopled predominantly by Kurds who, although Muslims, had their own language and culture.

Under the terms of the Sykes–Picot agreement, the Mosul governate was to have gone to France. However, the French eventually abandoned their claim in favour of the British in 1920, a year which saw separate revolts by both Kurds and Arabs against British rule.

59

The British did not consider the Arab provinces of Mesopotamia to be a self-supporting state and therefore insisted on the inclusion of Mosul, where the bulk of the region's oil wealth was at that time believed to be concentrated. In November 1920 Mosul was annexed to the two southern governates and a year later the Hashemite Emir, Faisal, who had been turned out of Damascus by the French after they crushed his Arab administration, was installed under British tutelage as King of Iraq. The Kurdish independent leader, Sheikh Mahmoud, who had declared himself King of Kurdistan, was deported to India. The post-war Treaty of Sèvres, which in 1920 had promised the Kurds an independent state, was never ratified, though Turkey, which had fostered unrest among the Kurds as a means of pressing its own claim to Mosul, did finally accede to its incorporation into Iraq in 1926 in return for a stake in the new state's oil revenues. King Faisal mounted the throne of a state which was not only an artificial creation of the colonial powers but also culturally, religiously and even linguistically heterogeneous.

The bulk of the population of the south were Shia Muslims, a minority of the whole population were Sunni; the Kurds, while also Sunni, were not Arabs and aspired to a state of their own. The economic infrastructure was semi-feudal, dominated by tribal Arab sheikhs in the south and centre, and by hereditary 'aghas' in the Kurdish north. And real political power, of course, resided with the British, exercised by the high commissioner, Sir Percy Cox, the architect of the new state.

Britain's interests in its troublesome new protectorate lay in safeguarding its oil concessions against competition from the Americans and others, maintaining mainland military bases east of Suez and protecting the approaches to India. There was no desire to maintain a long-term colonial presence in the new Iraq but rather to ensure continued British influence, if possible without the expense of maintaining a standing army there. While unrest was vigorously repressed by the British, patronage was at the same time used to establish a pro-British network of tribal sheikhs. Military control of the country was made the responsibility of the Royal Air Force, reflecting the emerging doctrine that air power, rather than ground forces, was the simplest, cheapest and often the most effective method of counter-insurgency. Air power was found to be particularly appropriate against the rebellious Kurds of the mountainous north, as Saddam Hussein was to find in his own Kurdish counter-insurgency campaign more than fifty years later. The RAF set a precedent for subsequent dictators by bombing and destroying entire Kurdish villages, a campaign in which Britain's wartime Bomber Command chief Air Marshal Arthur 'Bomber' Harris was involved. Unlike Saddam, the British did not use chemical weapons; but they developed instead the equally effective time-delayed bomb which would explode after fleeing peasants had ventured back to their gutted villages.

The Anglo–Iraqi Treaty of January 1926 established Britain's mandate over Iraq for twenty-five years, although there was a clause which allowed for full independence at an earlier date than 1951 should the new state gain admission to the League of Nations. Once Britain had succeeded in incorporating Mosul into the country, King Faisal and his government, including nationalist-minded former Arab officials of the Ottoman administration, were eager to press for early independence. But this did not prevent the emergence of popular, republican resentment against the monarchy, which most regarded as a tool of the British empire. Unrest grew after the signing in 1930 of a new Anglo–Iraqi treaty and the granting of further oil concessions to the British-owned Iraq Petroleum Company (IPC) to exploit vast, newly-discovered deposits near the northern town of Kirkuk.

Nationalists viewed the terms of the 1930 treaty as wholly beneficial to Britain and totally detrimental to the interests of Iraq. The signing was a prelude to the granting of full independence in 1932, the year of Iraq's admission to the League of Nations, but Britain maintained a neo-colonialist relationship with the new state until the revolution which toppled the monarchy and the pro-British ancien régime in 1958.

After 1932, the Iraqi army was enlarged by the introduction of conscription and began to emerge as an important element in the country's politics as younger nationalist officers found inspiration in the fascist dictatorships of Germany and Italy. The army gained added popularity by its slaughter in 1933 of the rebellious Christian Assyrian community which had stayed loyal to the British in the 1920 Arab revolt in southern Iraq. It was the first of the pogroms and massacres which were to stain the history of modern Iraq and it established a tradition of political brutality which was faithfully followed by Saddam Hussein.

Anti-Semitism also featured on Iraq's new political agenda. Encouraged in the name of anti-Zionism, it was a strong feature of Baathist rule after 1968. Early the following year, the hanged corpses of Jewish 'spies' were left dangling in Liberation Square to excite the hatred of the crowds.

In 1933 King Faisal died and was replaced by his son, Ghazi, who was killed in a road accident in 1939. He was succeeded by a regent who ruled on behalf of his four-year-old son, Faisal, while real political power resided with the pro-British politician, Nuri Said, a former Ottoman officer who was the effective strongman of Iraq until the 1958 revolution. It was nevertheless an era of coups and counter-coups mounted by the evolving politico-military class. The first takeover was in 1936, staged by Bakr Sidqi, one of the butchers of the Assyrian community, and there were five more coups before the outbreak of the Second World War.

In April 1941, pro-Axis officers and nationalist politicians under the leadership of Rashid Ali al-Gailani staged a revolt against continued British hegemony and challenged Britain's right, under the 1930 treaty, to maintain troops on Iraqi territory. Nuri Said and the royal family were forced to flee the country until the uprising was suppressed by British force of arms. The revolt had the support of both the Nazis and Vichy France; in the same year British troops entered Syria from Palestine to oust the pro-Axis Vichy administration in Damascus.

The French writer Benoist-Mechin recalled in 1958 how he had helped to arrange the transfer of planes from Nazi Germany to Iraq to assist the Rashid Ali revolt. 'It was one of the reasons I was condemned to death,' wrote the author. 'Rashid Ali was also sentenced to capital punishment. Thus he in Baghdad and I in Versailles were faced with the same penalty and for the same reason – for having opposed the schemes of Britain.' In Damascus, the Baath party was born out of an aid committee set up by Aflaq and Bitar to assist Rashid Ali's short-lived revolt.

In the early years of the war, when Germany appeared to be in the ascendant and America had yet to join the allied cause, it was perhaps inevitable that nationalists in the Middle East should look to the Nazis as natural partners in the struggle against British domination. But after the allied victory at El Alamein in November 1942, the tide of war in the Middle East turned against Germany and two months after that battle, Iraq declared war on Germany.

Rashid Ali escaped to Saudi Arabia and from there to Berlin. After the war, he continued to denounce those who had collaborated with the British as traitors and to describe his relationship with his country in nationalist–romantic terms which later found an echo in the mythologizing rhetoric of the Saddam regime. 'I belong to the ancient line of the Gailani,' said Rashid Ali in an interview shortly before the 1958 revolution. 'My ancestor is buried at the golden mosque of Qadimain. I am at home in Baghdad, while the Hashemites, brought up from the Hejaz by British bayonets, are merely intruders.'

Rashid Ali's revolt in 1941 gave an active expression to the nationalist ideas being propagated by Aflaq and Bitar. After the two men returned from the Sorbonne they were employed at the main secondary school in Damascus, where Aflaq taught history and Bitar science. The Damascus schools were a hotbed of political conflict and intrigue in the uncertain war years, with demonstrations frequently turning into riots against the occupying French. Rival parties promoting a variety of nationalist and anti-colonialist solutions organized their own militias and youth groups. The Communists preached socialist internationalism, while the Muslim Brotherhood campaigned for the creation of a pure Islamic state, purged of Western influence; the Christian nationalist, Antun Saada, called for the creation of a Greater Syria encompassing the entire Levant, while Zaki Arsuzi, another Sorbonne graduate, laid the theoretical groundwork for a modern Arab renaissance. Aflaq and Bitar set up a nationalist study group in 1940 which they named the Movement of Arab Revival. Inspired by the example of Rashid Ali in Iraq the following year, they renamed it the Baath (renaissance) movement, with the slogan 'Unity, Freedom, Socialism'.

Despite its pan-Arabist message and branches in every Arab state, the Baath only ever came to power in Syria and neighbouring Iraq, where the doctrines of the movement had been spread by Syrian teachers in the late 1940s. An Iraqi branch of the party was established by Fuad al-Rikabi in 1952 and began to attract members away from the rival revolutionary movement, the Communist party. When Saddam Hussein joined the party in 1957, it had been active in Iraq for only five years. Unlike Syria, where the Baathists struggled for power in the streets with the conservative Muslim Brotherhood, Iraq saw a conflict between Baathists and Communists. The Communist Party in Iraq was the largest in the Middle East: its doctrine appealed both to the poor Shia of the south, who were separated from the Arab mainstream by their religion, and to Kurds and other ethnic minorities who were separated from the Arab state by their race.

The allied victory in the war meant that the Middle East emerged from the conflict with its map unchanged. Syria and Lebanon gained their independence from France and the new Labour government in Britain, economically weakened by six years of war, wanted to scale down its Middle Eastern commitments. But as the era of the Cold War dawned it was deemed necessary to maintain a British presence in the region in order to provide a bulwark along the southern flank of the Soviet Union and to prop up pro-Western regimes, including that in Iraq, which could now be relied upon to suppress Communist agitation.

After the war, Baghdad sought a renegotiation of the deeply unpopular 1930 Anglo–Iraqi treaty. Nationalists sought to end the provisions which allowed the continued maintenance of British bases on Iraqi soil but the pro-British Nuri Said, working behind the scenes, ensured that the revised treaty, signed at Portsmouth on

15 January 1948, left most of Britain's rights intact. Publication of the treaty led to strikes and demonstrations in Baghdad, supported by the main opposition parties. The unrest was ruthlessly repressed, with several hundreds killed by troops and police dispatched on to the streets with machine guns by Nuri Said. However, the prospect of a social revolution and the threat it posed to the monarchy frightened the regent, Abdul Illah, into appointing a new government whose first act was to reject the humiliating treaty signed only two weeks earlier at Portsmouth.

Although 1948 saw this small victory for nationalists in Iraq, it was also the year of the 'catastrophe' of the Arab nation as a whole. In May, British forces withdrew from Palestine and the Jewish population declared the independent state of Israel on the territory allotted to it by the United Nations. The Arab chiefs of staff had already determined on a strategy to stifle the new state at birth in a co-ordinated attack by the Iraqi, Syrian, Lebanese, Transjordanian and Egyptian armies. But the new state fought off the combined armies of its Arab neighbours and, in doing so, enlarged its territory. Britain, which took a broadly pro-Arab stance in view of its relations with its Middle Eastern client states, was forced by American pressure to stop arms supplies to the Arabs. Not only had the Arabs suffered the first of many humiliating defeats at the hands of Israel but also, in the hour of need, the old colonial master, Britain, had deserted them.

From 1948, the conflict with Israel became the touchstone of Arab politics and the 'liberation' of Arab land the rallying cry of both patriots and charlatans who hoped to exploit the festering resentment of the Arabs for their own ends. The events of 1948 fed the nationalist fervour of young officers in the Arab world who blamed the corruption of their reactionary regimes for the failure to defeat the new Jewish state.

A veteran of the 1948 war, Gamal Abdel Nasser, led the 1952 revolt which ousted the Egyptian monarchy of King Farouk and instituted a revolutionary, republican regime. Nasser's challenge to the European powers in the Suez crisis of 1956 reverberated throughout the Arab world; it further damaged the prestige of

Britain and France and gave the Soviet Union a doorway into the Middle East, the very thing that the Western presence in the region had been designed to prevent. From then on the Soviet Union became identified as the supporter of Arab nationalism against the vested interests of the neo-colonialist West.

Nasser posed a threat not only to Western interests but also to pro-Western regimes in the Middle East. This threat increased after the creation of the United Arab Republic on 1 February 1958 which unified the regimes of Egypt and Syria. The union had been sought by the Syrian Baathists who felt that Nasser's prestige would counter the growing influence of the Communists there. The union appeared to be yet another inspirational step along the path of Arab renaissance and, to friend and foe alike, the Nasserite tide appeared unstoppable.

In 1954, the pro-Western Iraqi, Nuri Said, had tried unsuccessfully to persuade Nasser to bring Egypt into a Western-sponsored alliance designed to secure the Middle East against Soviet expansionism. The first element of the alliance was already in place by February that year when Pakistan and Turkey signed a mutual defence pact. Nuri Said had been an officer in the Turkish army, captured by the British in the Basra campaign in the First World War, but he had since come to regard the relationship with Britain as the key to Iraqi foreign policy. He saw the Soviet Union as Iraq's natural enemy. Nasser, too, was an anti-Communist but he believed that the real Soviet threat was of internal subversion which could only be combated by improving the lot of the Arab masses. He had, in any case, defied the Western powers by purchasing arms from the Soviet bloc.

Nasser declined to join the new alliance and in February the following year Iraq went its own way by signing a defence treaty with Turkey, the foundation stone of what became known as the Baghdad pact including Iran, Pakistan, the United States and Britain. Iraq's membership of the pact created an irrevocable rift with Egypt and was viewed by nationalists at home as yet another surrender to Western interests. Nuri Said's reputation was further damaged when it was revealed that he had conspired with the

British before the Suez crisis to plot the overthrow of Nasser. These factors helped to sow the seeds of the revolution of 1958, as did Nuri Said's creation of the so-called Arab Federation between Jordan and Iraq, presided over by the Hashemite monarchs, Faisal II and Hussein, a conservative reaction to the setting up of the United Arab Republic.

Nuri Said was firmly opposed to the theories of the pan-Arabists, although his view of Iraq's role in the Arab world was remarkably similar to that espoused much later by Saddam Hussein. In an interview shortly before the 1958 revolution, Nuri said: 'For centuries Baghdad has been the capital of the Arab world. Remember the Abassid empire. It also stretched from the Atlantic to the Persian Gulf. What am I saying? Much further, since it reached as far as India ... It's up to Iraq to assume the leadership of the Arab world. I wouldn't like to depart before having achieved that. But many dangers stalk us. In Cairo, they talk a lot about pooling the resources of the Middle East, of sharing out the oil revenues according to population ...'

Within three months, Nuri Said was dead. Dressed as a woman, the old man had tried to flee to safety on 16 July, two days after the Free Officers movement of Brigadier Qassem and Colonel Abdel Salam Aref had led the army into Baghdad. Despite his disguise, Nuri Said was recognized and, realizing he could not escape, he pulled out his revolver and shot himself. At dawn on the morning of the revolution, the royal palace was surrounded; the king and the regent, Prince Abdul Illah, believing their lives would be spared if they surrendered, allowed the rebels to escort them into the front courtyard. There, they were shot dead.

This July revolution was the watershed in modern Iraqi history. The Republic of Iraq was established by Proclamation One of 14 July 1958, and news of the death of the king prompted a popular uprising. The proclamation brought thousands of people, including peasants and nomads, into the city where they were urged on by young militants of the nationalist and leftist parties to attack anyone who might be associated with the old regime, including foreigners. The body of Abdul Illah was turned over to the crowd who mutilated it and dragged it through the streets, and on 17 July the mob discovered the burial place of Nuri Said and set fire to his body in front of the Egyptian embassy.

In the months leading up to 14 July, Iraq had been in a state of pre-revolutionary turmoil. Even the British embassy had made a desultory effort to warn the old regime that failure to improve social conditions for the poor would lead to an explosion of unrest, but Nuri Said's government was unmoved; although he prided himself on the dams and irrigation systems which had begun to improve agricultural output, most of the benefits went straight to the feudal sheikhs who ruled the countryside. By 1958, the old regime was quite out of tune with the nationalist aspirations of the young and of the officer corps.

But although Iraq was in a mood for revolutionary change it was divided by conflict between different cultural and ethnic groups. After twenty-six years of nominal independence, the country had yet to take on the attributes of a nation-state. The nationalists were divided between those who wished to build a separate Iraqi state and the pan-Arabists, who viewed Iraq as part of a future Arab superstate. The Kurds, as non-Arabs, were among the most ardent partisans of the Iraqi nation-state since they saw no benefits in pan-Arabism. The Shia had reservations about pan-Arabism since the numerical advantage they enjoyed within the borders of Iraq would disappear if the country were to be incorporated into the wider, and predominantly Sunni, Arab state. The Shia were attracted to pan-Arabism only insofar as it was opposed to the old Sunni oligarchy which had kept the social structure of the Ottoman empire intact.

The pan-Arabist doctrines of the Baath, however, attracted poor and radically-minded Sunni Arabs, such as Saddam Hussein, who did not enjoy a stake in the pre-1958 regime. Just as the minority Alawites embraced Baathism in Syria, so did the minority Sunni Arabs embrace it in Iraq. Thus, in the early 1950s, Baathism made inroads in the Sunni heartland north of Baghdad, in towns such as Samarra and Felluja and Saddam's hometown of Takrit.

At the time of the 1958 revolution, however, the Iraqi Baath was still little known. A veteran of that era, who preferred to remain anonymous, recalled how four parties gathered secretly in 1957 to sign the charter of a national front opposed to the monarchy and Nuri Said. 'The signatories were the National Democratic Party, the Istiqlal or Independence Party and the Communists; and then there was the signature of Fuad al-Rikabi for the Baath Arab Socialist Party. At that time people had never heard of them.'

The first two signatory parties operated openly before the revolution, despite periodic repression, but the two radical groups in the alliance, the Communists and the Baathists, had never been officially recognized. At the time it is unlikely that Baath membership amounted to more than a few hundred, though it was attracting interest among the young and the dispossessed who had previously been drawn to leftist politics. This rivalry for support was to mark the later conflicts between Baathists and Communists. Baathism was a movement, according to its critics, which attracted outsiders and misfits and those who saw violence as a path to political power.

Not that the Baathists had a monopoly of violence during the Qassem regime. The Communists, who put their resources behind President Qassem, despite his occasional efforts to restrain them, imposed a reign of terror against their opponents through domination of the Popular Resistance Force. This volunteer militia was set up within two weeks of the revolution, ostensibly as a civil defence force which would help the regular military forces to maintain order. It rapidly developed into a storm troop of the left, with its members invading private homes and beating and arresting political opponents. The Communists infiltrated the militia at an early stage and Qassem used it as a weapon to deal with those he saw as his main enemies – the Baathists and other pan-Arabists. Another instrument of repression set up by the revolution was the Mahdawi Court – the military tribunal which later tried and sentenced Saddam's comrades for their part in the 1959 assassination attempt against Qassem.

Within a year of the overthrow of the monarchy, those who had participated in that enterprise – the Communists and the pan-Arabists – were at each other's throats in a virtual civil war. The preference for violence over debate in post-revolutionary politics well suited young militants, such as Saddam, who were prepared to attack and kill on behalf of their chosen party.

The reason for the split between the Communist-backed Qassem and the pan-Arabists was that the latter had wrongly assumed that the revolution would lead to the speedy creation with Egypt and Syria of an enlarged United Arab Republic. The Communists, whose international aspirations were not limited to the confines of the Arab world, had no interest in pan-Arabism; Qassem, for his part, soon made it clear that he put the interests of Iraq above those of a putative united Arab state. In any case, he had no intention of being overshadowed by Nasser, as he would have been had Iraq joined the UAR.

Although Aflaq's Baathist leadership in Syria had encouraged the union between Egypt and Syria, the price it had to pay was the voluntary dissolution of the party under pressure from Nasser. The Egyptian leader's brand of pan-Arabism expressed itself in a total mistrust of political parties; he was as anti-Baathist as he was anti-Communist. Aflaq and his colleagues on the right of the party agreed to commit political suicide for the sake of the union, much to the distress of younger, more radical men in the movement, such as the future Syrian president, Hafez al-Assad. This was at the heart of the dispute which was later to split the party into rival Iraqi and Syrian wings and to condemn its founder, Michel Aflaq, to die in exile.

The collapse of the Baathist national leadership in Damascus left the militants in Baghdad to confront the repression of Qassem and the Communists on their own. The founder of the Iraqi party, Rikabi, was among those behind the assassination plot against Qassem. He opened a Pandora's box of political violence from which emerged Saddam Hussein; Rikabi himself was to become one of the innumerable victims.

In the first year of the revolution, before the split between Qassem and his pan-Arabist military partner, Colonel Aref, Rikabi had been appointed to the cabinet as development minister. Later he fell out with other Baath leaders and abandoned the party in

1961 to align himself with the Nasserites. After the Baathists were toppled from power in 1963, he was again invited to join the cabinet. Saddam typically did not forgive his treachery: in 1969, Rikabi was sentenced to one and a half years imprisonment which he was made to serve among the most violent common criminals. A former Baathist recalls how, two days before he was due to be released, 'the authorities brought in a hooligan armed with a knife. Rikabi was stabbed in the chest and then dragged on foot to the hospital. They left him unattended until he died.'

After the Saddam–Bakr partnership came to power in 1968, the original Baathist ideals of pan-Arabism began to take second place to a policy of Iraqi nationalism of the kind for which the Baath had once execrated President Qassem. Henceforward Iraq was ascribed a leadership rather than a partnership role in fulfilling Saddam's personal vision of the modern Arab state. 'We must make this country the solid base and living pillar of the whole Arab struggle, an example which will shine throughout the Middle East,' Saddam said in a speech as vice-president in 1974. 'It will not be an easy path.'

At the time of the 1968 Baathist coup, Saddam was only thirty-one and yet in a short time he made himself the most powerful man in Iraq. He had no intention in the long run of taking second place to either Bakr or any other leader of the Arab world. If the Arabs were to be reunited, it would be under his direction.

The 1968 coup prompted an undeclared civil war between the Baathists and their Communist rivals, marked by assassinations and car bombings. But as relations began to improve with the Soviet Union and the Eastern bloc, a truce was called and the Communists were invited into a ruling National Front as junior partners. 'What benefits did the Iraqi people gain from the old days when we were cutting each other's throats?' Saddam asked his new comrades. The Baath retained the commanding role in government and banned all political organization within the armed forces, except by the Baath. The alliance was little more than a Baathist trick to emasculate their main internal rivals, as the Communists were to learn to their cost within just a few years.

Communist participation in government nevertheless drew criticism from the West, to which Saddam responded by promoting hostility towards 'imperialism'. It was a period in which Iraq came to be regarded as the most radical and uncompromising Arab state, allied to Moscow and spearheading the opposition to a peace settlement with Israel. This perception was fed by Saddam's rhetoric. 'We are the kind who, the harder you hit us, the harder we hit back,' he stated in 1974. 'We are not the kind to allow ourselves to be besieged behind our walls.' He told the National Front: 'There is one thing that gives honour to us and to the Iraqi people and that is that imperialism is discomfited by the direction we have taken, discomfited by this country of ten million people, this little country in the Middle East.'

But as Saddam headed inexorably towards war with Iran, the rhetoric subtly changed. The strategic flirtation with Marxism was brought to an end and Saddam's message began to evoke more strongly than ever the primacy of Iraq within the wider Arab nation.

'The Arab nation is the source of all prophets and the cradle of civilization,' he said in an interview shortly after he assumed the presidency in 1979. 'And there is no doubt that the oldest civilization in the world is that of Mesopotamia. It is not an Iraqi civilization in isolation from the Arab nation. It is a civilization which developed thanks to the strength and ability of the Iraqi people, coupled with the efforts and heritage of the nation.'

If history was one element of the Saddam mythology, religion was another. Iraq was above all a secular state, in which, moreover, Saddam had repressed Islamic political movements both during and after the Gulf war. But Saddam turned increasingly to evocations of Iraq's glorious Islamic past. A much publicized pilgrimage to Mecca and the forgery of his family tree to show his descent from the Prophet were among the tactics he used to pose as an Islamic leader and further to establish his legitimacy. The Iranian revolution and the movements it inspired elsewhere in the Muslim world showed Saddam the benefits of harnessing religion to his cause; his efforts to link his family to the house of the Prophet were designed to appeal to the Shia, who respect the hereditary principle within Islam. The rhetoric he employed after his invasion of Kuwait was that of Islam rather than of the secular anti-imperialist struggle. The war of liberation was now to be a holy war. History was rewritten in the service of the state.

In this enterprise, Michel Aflaq served Saddam in death as he had in life: after his body was returned to Iraq it was announced by Baghdad that the venerable Christian founder of the secular Arab Baath Socialist Party had, on his death bed, converted to Islam.

The War That Never Ended

The invasion of Kuwait was the next step along the road to regional supremacy and Arab leadership for Saddam Hussein after his self-proclaimed victory over Iran two years earlier. He glorified the eight-year Gulf war, in which one million people were killed or wounded, as the second Qaddissiyeh, after the seventh-century battle in which the forces of Islam had defeated the Persian forces of Rustam.

In a speech marking the second anniversary of the ceasefire and delivered five days after his army's entry into Kuwait on 2 August, Saddam told the nation:

> While the second of August came as a legitimate offspring to the second Qaddissiyeh Battle and its people, and while it will be, with God's help, a faithful offspring . . . it will be the beginning of a new proud and rising stage. In that stage the horizons of virtue in various parts of the Arab homeland will widen in the coming days and filth, treachery and vileness, betrayal and subordination to the foreigner will retreat. Many of the Arabs' goals will come closer after it seemed to some people that they have gone far from their positions in the horizon. Suns will rise, moons will shine and the stars will glitter. The light will force darkness out and there will be no eclipse in the sky of Iraq and the Arab homeland.

After the longest conventional war between sovereign states of the twentieth century, Iraq might have seized the opportunity the 1988 ceasefire offered for a compromise peace. Instead, Saddam presented himself as the victor and delayed all the items in United Nations Resolution 598 except the call for a ceasefire, hoping to

improve his position as time went on. He had two main considerations in mind: first, he hoped to impose on Iran the border he
wanted, which would give Iraq control of the Shatt al-Arab right up
to the Iranian ports; second, he wanted to avoid that section of the
resolution which called for a commission to establish who was
responsible for the opening of hostilities. By removing the possibility of being blamed, he would also avoid the danger of being
ordered to pay reparations.

By proclaiming himself victor Saddam was also able to pose as
the saviour of the Arab Gulf and to remind states such as Kuwait
that, without him, they would have been overrun by the Persian
hordes; if they had been willing to finance him during the war, then
all the more reason why they should pay for his protection now that
he had won it.

Yet the war had really ended in a draw, with the opposing forces
virtually back to where they had started in September 1980. This
suited the major powers very well, as after failing in the first seven
years to halt the conflict, they had resolved in the eighth that it
should end with neither a winner nor a loser. A British parliamentary committee referred, in an official report of June 1988, to 'a
war which few want either side to win'.

Saddam had launched the war with the intention of filling the
power vacuum in the Gulf created by the fall of the Shah in January
1979. Until the overthrow of the monarchy, Iran was too powerful
to challenge; but with the coming of Ayatollah Khomeini's regime
and the apparent collapse of the Iranian armed forces, Saddam
believed the time had come to replace Iran as the power in the Gulf.

He had at least tacit American support for this enterprise as well
as the active backing of some of the Shah's former generals. Iraq
drew up a plan to stage a blitzkrieg into a large area of western Iran
and to bring in an Iranian royalist army which had assembled inside
Iraq. The invaders would then invite Shahpour Bakhtiar, the
Iranian prime minister ousted in 1979, to form a provisional
government under Iraqi tutelage. The former Iranian president,
Abolhassan Bani-Sadr, told the authors after the war that the plan
had been discussed with the Americans and had their approval. He

said that in the summer of 1980 he received intelligence reports of a meeting in Jordan between Saddam and President Carter's national security adviser, Zbigniew Brzezinski, in which the American was said to have pledged US backing for an attack on Iran.

US Gulf policy was in tatters by mid-1980. America had lost its policeman in the Gulf with the fall of the Shah and had failed in its efforts to establish a working relationship with his successors. On the contrary, the Tehran regime was virulently anti-Western and Khomeini's followers had provoked a complete break with Washington by seizing the US embassy and holding its diplomats hostage.

On the one hand, Khomeini appeared to threaten other pro-Western regimes in the Gulf through the export of Islamic fundamentalist revolution, while, on the other, the instability of the new regime in Tehran seemd to offer an ominous invitation to the Soviet Union to meddle further in Gulf affairs. In those circumstances, Saddam Hussein, so recently established as the unchallenged ruler of Iraq, and having apparently abandoned his anti-Western radicalism, seemed to be the lesser evil.

Among Saddam's war aims was to take and hold the southern Iranian border province which the Iranians call Khuzestan and the Iraqis Arabistan, and to incorporate it – Kuwait-like – into Greater Iraq. The people of the province were predominantly Arab; their territory therefore was to be considered Arab land and was shown as such on Iraqi maps. The incorporation of Khuzestan would have given Saddam the access to the Gulf he sought in addition to a buffer zone with Iran. In their failed blitzkrieg, however, Iraqi forces did not manage to capture any significant town in the province apart from the frontier port of Khorramshahr, temporarily restored to its old Arab name of Mohammarah.

By 1982, the Iranians had reversed the tide of war and by the summer of that year Iranian forces arrived on Iraqi territory. The prevalent view among other countries, including the conservative Arab states of the Gulf, was that Iran had effectively won the war, although a final peace might be some way off. On 26 October, Saddam announced that he accepted the frontier line in the Shatt

The Iraqi president is supremely conscious of his image. Seen here at the third Islamic Summit Conference in January 1981, he sports the gold-trimmed robe of an Arab potentate and an outsized cigar.

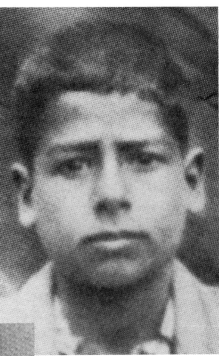

Saddam Hussein, pictured above in the late 1940s, had a miserable and lonely childhood in the provincial backwater of Takrit. His first possession was a revolver given to him when he was ten by his cousins. Later, in Baghdad, he turned to political violence, and took part in the 1959 assassination attempt on President Qassem. He is pictured left wearing the bedouin disguise in which he escaped to Syria after the shooting.

Top As vice-president from 1968 to 1979, Saddam became the strongman of
Iraq. Here, he and his three eldest children, posing for an official portrait in
1972, are overlooked by a painting which shows Saddam in the shadow
of President Ahmed Hassan al-Bakr, the distant relative whom he was to
oust in 1979.

Above Although Saddam's regime is secular, he played the Islamic card during
the Gulf war, in part to win the loyalty of the devout Shia masses, and made a
much-publicized pilgrimage to Mecca.

Top The evocation of Iraq's former glory became a central element of Saddamist mythology after the Gulf war. Saddam consciously compared himself with Nebuchadnezzar, the Babylonian king who captured Jerusalem and forced the Jews into exile.

Above By the end of the 1980s central Baghdad was dominated by huge monuments recording Iraq's self-proclaimed victory in the war. This 150-feet-high representation of twin shields rising from the ground, which was reputed to have cost a quarter of a billion dollars, is dedicated to the war dead.

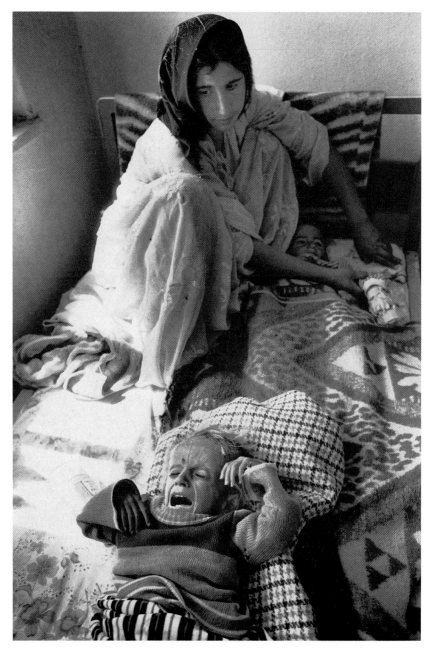

In late 1988, some 100,000 Kurds were forced to flee northern Iraq in the face of chemical weapon attacks. This woman and her child, who was badly gassed, were among those cared for in camps in southern Turkey.

Top The emir of Kuwait escaped at the start of the invasion and established his government in exile at the Saudi resort of Taif. Here, with his prime minister, Prince Saad, he greets the US secretary of state, James Baker.

Above Faced with grave economic problems by 1990, Saddam saw Kuwait as a treasure chest to be plundered. The gold souk, a symbol of Kuwait's opulance before the invasion, was one of the first places to be looted.

In the months before the invasion a new Arab axis emerged grouping King Hussein of Jordan, Yasser Arafat of the PLO and Saddam Hussein, pictured here in a Palestinian propaganda poster against the background of the Dome of the Rock in Jerusalem.

The Kuwait crisis broke in mid-summer, just as President Bush was due to start his annual golfing holiday at Kennebunkport in Maine. He went anyway, prompting the criticism from some that he should have stayed at his desk. His firm handling of the crisis in its early days, however, helped to bury the 'wimp factor'.

The United States poured almost half its army into the Gulf to confront the Iraqi threat. Troops from the 1st Cavalry Division moved out across the Saudi Arabian desert on 4 November, after having been addressed by Secretary of State James Baker.

al-Arab as delineated in the 1975 Algiers agreement which he signed with the Shah – an agreement which he had publicly torn up five days before invading Iran. Conflicting theories were later put forward to explain Saddam's motives in offering such a potentially humiliating concession; either he had come to the likely conclusion that the Iranians were poised to overrun Iraq and that only a grand gesture could save his regime, or else he anticipated that the offer would be rejected by the Iranians and that, by thus exposing the intransigence of Khomeini, he would win increased international support for Iraq.

Khomeini did indeed reject the offer and continued to press for total victory and the overthrow of the 'ungodly' regime in Baghdad. Far from bringing about Saddam's downfall, Khomeini's fateful decision to pursue the war for six more fruitless years effectively ensured the survival of the Iraqi dictator and allowed him further to consolidate his rule, strengthen his armed forces and accelerate a policy of acquiring sophisticated weapons technology. This was all carried out with the approval and indeed the assistance of the Western and Soviet blocs both of which feared the unsettling spread of fundamentalism that would stem from an Iranian victory. Once Iranian troops were on Iraqi soil, Moscow resumed arms shipments to Iraq which had been suspended in 1980 and for as long as Iraqi troops were on Iranian territory; and Washington authorized the supply of US military satellite information to Baghdad.

When Saddam sent his tanks across the border on 22 September 1980 he had been planning his revenge against Iran for five years, dating from the OPEC meeting in Algiers in 1975 at which he had been obliged, out of weakness, to accept the Shah's terms for a border settlement in exchange for the suspension of Iranian support to a Kurdish guerrilla insurgency at that time threatening the Baghdad regime.

OPEC was concerned that the antipathy between Iran and Iraq was undermining the unity of the oil cartel just as it was emerging as a player on the international scene following the oil price explosion of the early 1970s. The Algerian president, Houari Boumedienne, sponsored two meetings between the Shah and

Saddam – at that time still officially vice-president – and a joint declaration followed on 6 March. A binding treaty between the two countries was signed in June; the Shah halted supplies to the rebellious Kurds and their insurgency in northern Iraq collapsed.

The dispute over the frontier between Arab and Persian lands, which the 1975 treaty was intended to resolve, had existed for some five centuries and the first attempt to resolve it was in 1639. Later, Russia and Britain tried to impose solutions which would serve their own imperial interests. A 1937 treaty between Tehran and Baghdad established Iranian sovereignty as far as the median line of the Shatt al-Arab outside the oil city of Abadan but, elsewhere along the estuary, shipping was obliged to hoist the Iraqi flag and pay dues to Iraqi customs. The Shah unilaterally revoked the 1937 treaty on 19 April 1969, nine months after the Baathist takeover in Baghdad. It was a warning to the new regime that the Shah intended to be undisputed master of the Gulf. Baghdad threatened retaliation but did not at that time have the ability to take action.

The Shah's action came in response to plans for a British military withdrawal from the Gulf. Britain had established a protectorate during the previous century and a half, guaranteeing regional security in its own interests and those of its Western allies in the Gulf. But on 16 January 1968, the British prime minister, Harold Wilson, announced that the government intended to withdraw its forces from east of Suez by December 1971. The end of British hegemony in the Gulf was a signal for the larger local states, principally Iran, Iraq and Saudi Arabia, to begin competing for supremacy.

The British withdrawal also confronted the United States with the dilemma of how to ensure the security of this area of vital strategic and economic interest. Wilson's January 1968 announcement was made against the advice of Washington, which urged Britain to delay withdrawal until the mid or late 1970s. At this time, the United States was deeply involved in Vietnam, where the Tet offensive had erupted the same month, and was in no position to make a direct military commitment to the Gulf to replace the

departing British forces. On the very day of the Wilson announcement, the State Department affirmed that the United States had no
plans to fill the vacuum that would be created by British withdrawal.

The shock of the British decision nevertheless forced the Americans, for the first time, to formulate a coherent policy for Gulf
security. Washington's principal concern was that the Soviet Union
would now be able to extend its influence in the region by supporting Arab radicals, and would thereby gain control of Middle East
oil.

The Americans resolved their dilemma by picking on the most
powerful state in the region, Iran, to act as the West's watchdog.
The policy of relying on an outside party to guarantee American
interests was enshrined in the so-called Nixon Doctrine of the early
1970s, in which President Richard Nixon confirmed America's
readiness to give economic and military assistance to those with
whom it had treaty commitments while relying on such states,
when they were threatened, to provide the manpower for their own
defence.

It was a role which the Shah was only too ready to assume, given
his own desire for mastery of the Gulf. Iran had an outstanding
territorial claim to Bahrain, which had once been part of the
Persian empire, and it coveted three islands in the Gulf – Abu
Musa, which it shared with Sharjah, and Great and Lesser Tumb.
The claim to Bahrain was eventually dropped, but as Britain withdrew, the Iranians occupied the islands, provoking a break in
relations with Iraq. Although the islands were in the lower Gulf, far
from Iraq, the Baathist regime decided to promote itself as the
protector of Arab lands in the area. At the Baath party's eighth
congress in Baghdad in January 1974 it was resolved that: 'The
responsibility of the Arab Baath Socialist Party towards the Arab
Gulf springs first and foremost from its national principles and
aims. Iraq being the largest Arab country in the area and the most
advanced, carries the main burden in safeguarding the area.'

The conservative states of the Gulf, including Saudi Arabia,
found themselves caught in the middle of this growing rivalry

between Iran and Iraq, both of which they feared and mistrusted. Iraq was a radical and Soviet-allied state which threatened the conservatives with internal unrest while Iran was an alien non-Arab power bent on dominating them. This Saudi distrust of Iran prevented the emergence of a conservative defensive partnership between Tehran and Riyadh which Washington would have liked.

Instead, the three largest states in the area entered into an arms race with the support of outside powers. Iran received almost unrestricted access to most modern US weaponry; Iraq responded by increasing its arms purchases from the Soviet bloc and France; while Saudi Arabia continued its purchases from the West. This process of rearmament was assisted by a massive influx of funds after the oil price explosion of 1973 and the necessity for the industrialized countries to supply the needs of the oil producers in order to recycle petrodollars. Weapons sales offered the tantalizing prospect of killing two birds with one stone – not only would they ensure that regional states had the means to guarantee their own security, they would also bring in export income to compensate for the increased expenditure on imported oil. In the ten years following Wilson's announcement of Britain's impending withdrawal from east of Suez, Iranian arms purchases rose sixteenfold, Iraq's sixfold and Saudi Arabia's twenty-threefold.

In 1974, Saddam took personal charge of a committee, which also included his brother-in-law, Chief of Staff Adnan Khairallah, established to look into ways of increasing Iraq's military potential, including the acquisition of chemical and nuclear weapons. The ostensible aim of this programme was to gain strategic parity with Israel; Iraq was among those states which rejected all compromise with the Israelis and, although not a frontline state, had sent forces to fight in the 1973 Middle East war. With the rise of Iranian power in the early 1970s, however, the Baathist regime was faced with a potential enemy much closer to home in the shape of Iran, and in the end the new weapons served not to defeat the Zionist enemy, but to confront the 'Persian racists' to the east. After the mid-1970s Iraq moved gradually away from its ultra-radical, anti-Zionist stance as its attention became focused on its role in the Gulf.

Although Saddam continued to preach pan-Arabism, his foreign policy took on an increasingly nationalist tinge.

After Britain's withdrawal from the Gulf, Moscow did indeed take opportunities for extending its influence in an area from which it had previously been excluded. Despite the ideological antipathy between Communism and the Baath, both sides saw advantages in an anti-Western alliance of convenience and in 1972 the two countries signed a fifteen-year Treaty of Friendship. The treaty provided the framework for close economic and military co-operation between the two countries but, ironically, it also prompted the United States and other Western states to renew their interest in closer ties with Baghdad in order to offset growing Soviet influence.

Nor were the Soviets totally dependable allies. Even before the Iranian revolution Moscow sought to increase its ties with Iran, a process which accelerated after the fall of the Shah. When Iraq invaded Iran, Moscow suspended weapons deliveries for almost two years until the invaders had withdrawn.

A much more consistent ally was France – until the invasion of Kuwait. On 21 August 1990, the Iraqi News Agency published a communiqué declaring the 'end of the friendship with France'. Until the previous day, France had been considered as a friend, the statement said regretfully, but its decision to join the American blockade put it on the same level as the United States. 'We call on the French people to resist the policy of their government which has declared war on a friendly state and people.'

The communiqué marked the end not so much of a friendship as of a love affair which had been established between the two countries over more than twenty years. During that period France became not only Iraq's biggest arms supplier after the Soviet Union but also the principal Western supporter and apologist of the Baathist regime. Other states might support Saddam for commercial or strategic reasons, but the French saw in him a Middle Eastern reflection of their own revolutionary ideals. This attitude found its most extreme advocate in the writer Charles Saint-Prot, who wrote: 'I have met him on frequent occasions. He is neither

Hitler nor the big, bad wolf. He is a Babylonian. This man has ten, fifteen thousand years of history behind him.'

France's inclination towards the Arab world was initiated by President Charles de Gaulle after the 1967 Six-Day war. De Gaulle, who had extricated France from a long and bloody colonial war in Algeria, regarded a closer relationship with the Arabs as one means of promoting a non-aligned foreign policy distinct from that of Britain and the United States. Saddam was an admirer of Charles de Gaulle, once referring to him as 'the knight whose chivalry I most admire'.

The relationship which grew up between the two countries was at one level an expression of mutual anglophobia. Iraq was not in the traditional French sphere of influence in the Middle East. It had been a virtual British fiefdom until the 1958 revolution, an event which happened, as the Iraqis never tired or reminding their French friends, on Bastille Day.

After the Baathist takeover in 1968, successive Gaullist governments, recognizing Baghdad's aspirations to a leading role in the non-aligned movement, viewed Iraq as a natural target for France's independent foreign policy. France therefore offered itself as a patron and supplier who could help Iraq avoid becoming over-dependent on the Soviet Union. The relationship grew closer still in the mid-1970s when, thanks to the huge increase in world oil prices, the Baathist regime at last had the means to buy the weapons and technology required for the construction of Saddam's modern Arab state. In 1975, the French prime minister, Jacques Chirac, paid an official visit to Iraq and Saddam visited France, his only visit to a Western country. It was the birth of a Franco–Iraqi 'special relationship' and of an era of huge armament and development projects in which Iraq became the focus of French policy in the Middle East.

The French came to regard Iraq as a thrusting and dynamic country which shared France's own republican and progressive ideals. There was a constant traffic of businessmen and contractors between Paris and Baghdad and a growth of cultural exchanges. In 1977, an Iraqi cultural centre was set up in a Paris building

belonging to the Dassault family, the founders of the French armaments firm which produced the Mirage fighter. As the relationship
grew, the excesses of the Saddam regime were dismissed as part of
the natural evolution of a revolutionary state.

From the start of the Gulf war in 1980, the French viewed
Saddam as a bulwark of modernism and secularism against the
obscurantist fundamentalism of Iran. The level of French arms
dealing initiated in the 1970s gathered pace in the next decade, and
in the first six years of the Gulf war, at which time Iraq began to run
into cash problems, French weapons transfers exceeded those of the
Soviet Union, amounting in value to $15–17 billion. In the same
period, the Iraqis spent an additional $5 billion on civilian and
commercial contracts with French firms. To the distress of the
Americans and the British, France even supplied Etendard jets and
Exocet missiles – the planes ostensibly on loan – which allowed
Iraq to plague Gulf shipping during the so-called tanker war.

France's most controversial deal, however, was the agreement
reached in 1975 to provide Iraq with a nuclear capacity. When it
published details of the agreement in the official gazette the following year, France insisted that the Osirak plant, fifteen miles outside
Baghdad, was destined for peaceful purposes. The deal had been
reached, however, under Saddam's personal supervision as part of
the programme he had headed since 1974 to obtain chemical and
nuclear weaponry that would assure strategic parity with Israel.
The Israelis certainly believed Osirak had military potential, for
they bombed and destroyed the site in June, 1981 during the first
year of the Gulf war.

Saddam had hoped that the special relationship with France was
strong enough to survive his invasion of Kuwait. Although the
relationship was the creation of the Gaullists, it had continued
when the socialists came to power; the socialist defence minister at
the time of the Kuwait invasion, Jean-Pierre Chevenement, had
been a founder member in 1984 of the Franco–Iraqi Friendship
Association.

But the public and political mood in France had changed by
1990. Iraq had run into difficulties with repayment of credits for its

vast arms purchases from France, and the mounting evidence of human rights abuses by the Saddam regime could no longer be dismissed as an expression of revolutionary zeal. A turning point came after the gassing of civilians in the Kurdish campaign of the summer of 1988. Danielle Mitterrand, wife of the French president, took up the cause of the Kurds under the aegis of her Association France-Libertés and organized a Kurdish conference in Paris in October 1989. The Iraqi foreign minister, Tareq Aziz, was to note later that 'since February, Iraq received negative signals concerning its relations with France'. Even so, the French government managed to delay the conference several times, arguing the need to avoid upsetting the Iraqis at a time when Baghdad had yet to pay its outstanding war debt of 32 billion francs.

Tareq Aziz was asked at the end of August by the French newspaper, *Le Figaro*, whether anything might yet be salvaged of the special relationship. He replied

> I have never asked France to side with us over Kuwait. But we had thought that she would conduct herself differently from the United States and Britain. Her attitude has shocked us. We now recall France's colonial past, whereas the Middle Eastern policy of de Gaulle, Pompidou, Giscard d'Estaing and even, at the beginning, of François Mitterrand, was clearly different from that of America . . .
>
> Today, we are seeing a confrontation at the heart of the Arab world: on the one side the independent forces of progress, on the other the corrupt and reactionary monarchies. France has made her choice.

Yet there was to be a further twist in the relationship between Iraq and France. Following a secret meeting in Tunis between Tareq Aziz and Claude Cheysson, the former foreign minister, Iraq agreed 'unconditionally' to release the 300-odd French hostages it was holding. France denied any deal had been made, but it was a clear indication of Iraq's determination to split the Western alliance opposed to it.

After the ceasefire of August 1988, the widespread perception was that Iran and Iraq, chastened and weakened by eight years of conflict, would now devote themselves to peaceful reconstruction. The industrialized countries, tempted by the prospect of lucrative peacetime contracts and the desire to cash in on the expected bonanza in the Gulf, were reluctant to criticize too vigorously the human rights record of either regime. Iraq was, in the West at least, considered to be a more reliable and worthwhile bet than Iran. True, Iraq had ended the war with enormous foreign debts, perhaps as high as $80 billion, but it appeared to be ruled by a stable if repressive régime which had thankfully put its radical past behind it. Besides, Iraq had the second highest oil reserves in the world after Saudi Arabia. Iran, despite a good credit record during the war, continued to be regarded as inherently unstable and anti-Western.

Saddam, moreover, had moved away from state monopolism and had, during the war, taken a number of steps to liberalize Iraq's economy and to permit the emergence of a new entrepreneurial class. Just after the war ended it was announced that, for the first time, the private sector was to be allowed to set up enterprises in direct competition with state industries. Saddam began to speak of the virtues of a pluralistic system in which the Baath would surrender its monopoly of Iraqi politics and in which, under a revised constitution, the president would share decision-making with the parliament and government. It was tempting, at the end of the 1980s, to imagine that Iraq would go the way of eastern Europe where economic and political liberalization seemed to be advancing hand-in-hand.

But economic problems were beginning to strain Saddam's 'iron fist, open hand' policy under which the tightly controlled populace at least had the compensation of having enough to eat – even during the war the average Iraqi diet had the highest calorific content of any in the Middle East. In the 1970s, as part of his modernizing strategy, Saddam had overseen a major revolution in the Iraqi economy; building on increased oil revenues, he injected $16 billion into new industries in order to diversify the economy and create new export markets, but these efforts were squandered in the Gulf war and by the late 1980s the only industry which counted was the military industry. Plants were turned over to the Military Industries Commission, headed by Saddam's cousin, Hussein Kamel Majid. When the war ended, Hussein Kamel was named as head of a new Military Industrialization ministry which was to combine the resources of military and civilian enterprises. Within a year of the ceasefire, in April 1989, Baghdad hosted its first military industries exhibition and announced plans to go into both missile and aircraft production.

By 1988, although Iraq had the fourth biggest army in the world, it also had an economy which was militarily oriented – and broke. Between the start of the war and the ceasefire an international glut had halved the nominal value of oil, and its real value was even lower. Furthermore, there was little prospect that Iraq's wartime backers, Saudi Arabia and Kuwait, would continue to prop up the Iraqi economy now that the war with Iran was over. At a summit of the Arab League in Baghdad in May 1990, Saddam complained that every $1 a barrel fall in the price of oil was costing Iraq $1 billion a year. By the time of the invasion of Kuwait the government had imposed hard currency limits on Iraqi companies, restricting their ability to buy spare parts and machinery from abroad.

By the end of the 1980s, Saddam's foreign policy seemed to have moved away from the radical camp and closer to moderate partners in the Arab world who had backed him against Iran. Before the war he had aspired to a world role through leadership of the non-aligned movement; he had hoped to host the group's 1982 summit as a Third World hero to outshine Nasser, Tito or Castro, but the course of the war forced the summit to be cancelled.

Now his aspirations appeared, on the surface, to be more modest. Thus, when Iraq announced its participation in a new regional grouping, the Arab Co-operation Council, alongside Egypt, Jordan and Yemen, this was taken as a sign that Iraq had finally abandoned aggressive pan-Arabism in favour of peaceful co-operation with like-minded moderate states.

The perception that Saddam was a reformed character overlooked the fundamental nature of his regime and the internal problems which it faced after the war. The eight-year conflict had drained Iraq's resources to the extent that it was forced to fall back on the old policy of expansionism to save it from economic disaster; it also left Iraq with a huge and highly advanced military–industrial infrastructure and an army of one million men who no longer had a war to fight.

Before long there were reports of unrest and lawlessness among demobilized and unemployed troops, some of whom turned to armed robbery. In mid-August 1989, a year after the ceasefire, fights broke out at the Baghdad bus station among about fifty armed soldiers recently demobilized from the border marshlands. Dozens of civilians were killed in the shooting but the authorities tried to cover up the affair to maintain the image of post-war tranquillity; it was announced that the police had opened fire on a gang of car thieves and unfortunately some people had died.

In this uncertain atmosphere Saddam was careful to ensure that none of the senior army officers who had gained popularity among their men during the war should have an opportunity to challenge him. In the autumn of 1988, two prominent wartime generals, Abdul Rashid and Salman Shuja, were killed in separate helicopter crashes and the following year, a number of Baathists and officers were executed for plotting a coup. In the marshes north of Basra, chemical weapons raids were used against Iraqi army deserters who had set up freebooting bands of brigands to prey on the surrounding countryside.

But nothing did more to expose the true nature of Saddam's regime than his treatment of the Kurds.

Although the Iranian-backed Kurdish insurgency had been defeated in 1975 and the Kurdish leader, Mulla Mustafa Barzani, had gone into exile, some fought on. In 1980, when the war with Iran began, the Kurds once more saw an opportunity to establish their national rights by mounting a guerrilla war against the Iraqi army. In this enterprise they once again received Iranian support, this time from the revolutionary regime of Ayatollah Khomeini.

It was not until the closing months of the war in 1988 that Saddam was able to wreak his vengeance upon the Kurds. By now he had added new weapons to his arsenal – chemical and nerve gasses. The attack on Halabja in March 1988 in which 5,000 civilians were killed was just the opening shot in a campaign against the Kurds which was to accelerate once the ceasefire came into force later that year. Halabja was the first time that Iraq had unleashed its chemical arsenal against civilian targets; it was also the first recorded use of nerve gas anywhere in the world.

But the official international response was muted. The UN powers were at that time trying to settle the Gulf war and hesitated to adopt a critical stance towards Iraq which might upset the delicate peace process. Saddam therefore felt free to pursue his campaign against the Kurds with relative impunity.

News of the post-war massacres nevertheless reached the outside world. A British documentary film-maker, Gwynne Roberts, was smuggled into Iraqi Kurdistan in September 1988 and brought back soil samples which proved the Iraqis had used mustard and nerve gas against Kurdish targets. He also interviewed survivors of an air attack on 28 August against Kurdish civilians, most of them women and children, in the Bassay gorge, twenty miles south of the Turkish border. Peshmerga fighters looked on helplessly from the hillsides as the planes attacked. One of them, Ramazan Mohammad, later told Roberts: 'There must have been 3,000 bodies and thousands of animals, all dead. The dead had a film over their eyes and out of their nose and from the sides of their mouth there was a horrible slime coming out. The skin was peeling and bubbling up.'

Alerted by reports coming out of Kurdistan, the chairman of the US Senate Foreign Relations Committee, Claiborne Pell, sent a two-man team to Turkey to investigate. The team members, Peter Galbraith and Christopher Van Hollen, reported back in October that Iraq was using chemical weapons as part of a policy to depopulate Kurdistan and to relocate the population elsewhere in Iraq. 'The end result of this policy will be the destruction of the Kurdish identity, Kurdish culture, and a way of life that has endured for centuries.' The report led Pell to introduce the

Prevention of Genocide Act 1988 for which he won unanimous approval. But the Reagan White House described the proprosed legislation as premature and counter-productive and succeeded in having the bill squashed in the run-up to the 1988 presidential election.

Most Western states paid lip service to the need to restrain Iraq's chemical weapons programme but this usually took the form of trying not to upset Baghdad. The American commentator, Milton Viorst, arguing against proposed sanctions against Iraq, wrote in September 1988: 'For America, the breakdown of ties contemplated in pending congressional bills would squander Iraq's rapprochement with the moderate Arab states, on which US Middle East policy is based. Instead there may emerge a volatile and chauvinistic Iraq which, with its powerful army and recent "victory", could threaten regional stability.'

In Britain, the government attacked Iraq's policy towards the Kurds and its use of chemical weapons in the campaign. But a Foreign Office briefing paper of September 1988 stated: 'We believe it better to maintain a dialogue with others if we want to influence their actions. Punitive measures such as unilateral sanctions would not be effective in changing Iraq's behaviour over chemical weapons, and would damage British interests to no avail.'

The Soviet bloc, despite the advent of Mikhail Gorbachev and perestroika, remained silent. The Kurdish Democratic Party sent an official to Prague for a meeting with Czech and Soviet officials and to ask for clarification of their stand on Iraq's chemical weapons' use. According to the KDP man, Hosha Zebari: 'I was told that anything that the United States got involved in, they would distance themselves from.'

Many in the Arab and non-aligned blocs were supportive of Saddam, to the extent that at the UN Human Rights Commission in Geneva his half-brother, Barzan Takriti, a former Baath intelligence chief turned diplomat, secured enough votes to have Iraq removed from the list of persistent human rights offenders.

Saddam's suppression of the Kurds was not purely an act of revenge for their pro-Iranian activities in the war; he also wished to establish a cordon sanitaire along Iraq's borders with Iran and Turkey, particularly if further military action in the Gulf was already being contemplated. The KDP leader Masoud Barzani, son of Mulla Mustafa, said that by mid-1989 Iraq had destroyed 4,000 settlements and villages in Kurdistan and that out of 75,000 square kilometres of traditional Kurdish land in Iraq, 45,000 had already been cleared of Kurds and resettled by Arabs, many of them Egyptian and Yemeni immigrants. Other areas were given over to secret military complexes such as a new plant in the Chira Gara mountains near Turkey where the Iraqis appeared, in 1990, to be setting up a uranium mine.

It was a bitter irony for the Kurds that, while Saddam pursued a policy which would inevitably lead to the eradication of their separate culture, he often posed in Kurdish dress and, as part of his self-glorification, frequently compared himself with the greatest of all Kurdish heroes, the scourge of Richard the Lionheart and the Christian crusaders – Saladin.

With hindsight, it is clear that the Western policy of appeasing Saddam was an error. The West should have been alerted as soon as it became apparent that Iraq was expanding its military infrastructure and researches once the war with Iran was over, rather than concentrating its resources on peaceful reconstruction. There was no evidence that Israel regarded Iraq as a target and Iran, the only other obvious enemy, was in no position to gather its forces for another war.

In October 1989, the Washington Institute for Near East Policy, a private research foundation, issued a report entitled 'The Genie Unleashed', which catalogued Iraq's chemical and biological weapons production and suggested that the West might already have lost the battle to halt proliferation of such weapons. The report stated that: 'Significantly, Iraq has continued and even expanded its efforts since the cessation of fighting with Iran in July 1988...'

The report said that international efforts to undermine the chemical weapons programme by starving it of raw materials were increasingly irrelevant as Iraq was on the verge of becoming self-sufficient. 'Baghdad's willingness to invest substantial resources in its chemical and biological weapons programs suggests that its leaders believe that these programs will continue to be of tremendous strategic importance,' the report said.

The threat from Iraq's biological weapons programme was largely overlooked despite reports that botulin toxin was being produced in military quantities and that a biological warfare research facility had been set up at Salman Park, twenty miles south-east of Baghdad. West German intelligence believed that the plant had been set up with the assistance of West German companies. Iraq's biological programme was ostensibly geared to peaceful research, aimed at the production of animal and human vaccines. But it was significant that a new State Enterprise for Drug Industries set up after the war at Samarra, where the main chemical weapons factory was situated, was placed under the auspices of the Military Industrialization ministry. The Iraqis were believed to be investigating the possible military applications of typhoid, cholera, anthrax, tularemia and equine encephalitis.

The virtue of developing chemical and biological weapons as a means to strategic parity, or even supremacy, in the Middle East, was that, by passing off the research facilities as part of the country's peaceful pharmaceutical industry, Iraq was able to attract credit from Western banks.

The Washington Institute for Near East Policy report concluded: 'The implication of these efforts remains uncertain, since rapid advances in biotechnology may make frightening innovations possible in toxin and biological agents. Should Iraq attempt to "weaponize" its biological agents, it would have the Third World's equivalent of nuclear weapons.'

As for nuclear weapons, the Western assumption was that Israel's air raid on the Osirak plant in 1981 had largely put paid to Iraq's nuclear ambitions. But soon after the invasion of Kuwait, intelligence sources began to speak of their fears that Iraq might be nearer than had been thought to producing a bomb and that Saddam might have an atomic weapons capability by the mid-1990s in the absense of more stringent measures to prevent the transfer of sensitive technology. This might have been dismissed as black propaganda had not the American and the British investigators uncovered in 1989 an Iraqi scheme to obtain electronic triggers, of the kind used in nuclear bombs, in violation of Western export controls. British customs searched an Iraqi airline bound for Baghdad and seized a number of krytrons – high voltage switches which can be used for detonating nuclear weapons. In fact, the switches were replicas, placed there by FBI and British customs agents who had been on to the Iraqi plan for several months.

Aside from its chemical weapons programme, there were also alarming indications of Iraq's advances in missile technology, another by-product of the war with Iran. During the war each side obtained missiles capable of reaching the other's capital; Egypt helped the Iraqis to develop an enhanced version of the Soviet-built Scud-B missile with a 180-mile range capable of hitting Tehran. Development also began on the Badr-2000, a 375-mile range missile based on the Argentine Condor-2. In December 1989, Iraq announced that it had launched a three-stage rocket capable of putting a satellite into space and had tested two missiles with a range of 1,200 miles. This was followed by an indirect warning from Saddam to Israel and the United States not to contemplate an attack on his missile facilities. Iraq would use 'all the means it possessed' to counteract attempts to attack its scientific and military achievements.

The weapons programme was by its very nature highly secretive, although it was accompanied by a publicity campaign which hinted at Iraq's advances in technology. But some unwelcome light was shed on the missile projects in September 1989 by reports of a huge explosion the previous month at a plant at al-Hillah, south of Baghdad. The first information about the disaster came from a Kurdish opposition group, Jalal Talabani's Patriotic Union of Kurdistan. The PUK said that many hundreds of people had been killed at a military-industrial complex at al-Hillah where the group claimed part of the missile programme was located. Foreign diplomats in Baghdad and US officials in Washington backed up the reports, prompting the Iraqis to issue a statement in which they referred to a relatively minor accident at a factory in which less than a score of people were killed.

The regime was clearly disturbed by the reports and may have suspected that sabotage was responsible for the 17 August explosion. Many Egyptians were employed in the missile programme and the cooling of relations between Cairo and Baghdad, as well as the start of a mass exodus of Egyptian workers from Iraq, dated from the explosion at al-Hillah.

By a fateful coincidence, a number of Western journalists had been invited to Iraq in early September to witness elections to a new Kurdish assembly, another element in Saddam's alleged post-war democratization programme but one which was widely regarded as a mere public relations exercise in view of the continuing conflict in the region. They included Farzad Bazoft, an exiled Iranian freelance journalist who worked for the *Observer* in London and had made previous trips to Iraq on the newspaper's behalf.

Bazoft arrived on the same day the al-Hillah reports broke in London and he decided to try to reach the plant to find out the details for himself. He was turned back the first time but returned the next day in the company of a British nursing administrator working in Baghdad, Daphne Parish, who agreed to drive him to the area. Copying the example of the journalist, Gwynne Roberts, in Kurdistan a year earlier, Bazoft collected some samples from the site, including a discarded shoe, apparently hoping to have them analysed later for traces of chemicals. He also spoke to a local man who confirmed that an explosion had taken place.

On 15 September, as he was about to board a plane home to London, Bazoft was arrested. Mrs Parish was arrested at her workplace four days later. In a subsequent televized confession clearly made under duress, Bazoft made the unconvincing admission that he had been working as a spy for Israel, apparently hoping that by confessing he would be treated leniently. It was not Saddam's way; throughout his rule he had used the tactic of extracting false confessions to justify the purging of his opponents. On 15 March 1990, after a one-day trial at which the prosecution failed to produce any convincing evidence of his guilt, Bazoft was shot dead by a firing squad. It was the beginning of the end of the West's relationship with 'moderate' Iraq.

There were many, however, who had an interest in not abandoning the relationship for the sake of a dead Iranian. By 1990 Britain was Iraq's third biggest trade partner and, in the week of Bazoft's trial, British banks were awaiting the result of a tender to raise a £250 million trade credit for Iraq. The credit had been granted in 1989 despite the fact that Bazoft and his friend, Mrs Parish, were already being held; nothing was to be done, it appeared, to prejudice British participation in the post-war reconstruction boom. It was also granted despite mounting concern about Iraq's ability to repay its debts. The British trade minister, Lord Trefgarne justified it on the grounds that it would open up 'new opportunities for British companies in this very important Middle East market'.

A small group of British MPs visited Baghdad while Bazoft and Parish were being held incommunicado. On his return from Baghdad, one of the Conservative MPs, Tony Marlow, wrote that Iraq was the victim of a 'vociferous and unrepresentative minority that affects to believe that our way of life and system of government is the measure by which all other countries should be measured'. As for British citizens who fell foul of the regime: 'No country can be expected to operate a differential system of justice in favour of foreigners.'

Shortly before Bazoft's execution, a British freelance journalist was contacted by a source on the fringes of British intelligence who informed him that Bazoft had a conviction in Britain for robbery and offered to supply copies of the charge sheets. This detail of Bazoft's past was already known to a small number of British journalists who considered it irrelevant to his current plight. While he was still alive, the story of his past conviction went unreported.

The day after his execution, however, rumours about his criminal past began to sweep Westminster and the Foreign Office press corps. As a consequence much of the subsequent press coverage centred on Bazoft's past rather than on his unfair trial and execution. Intelligence sources have since insisted that there was no co-ordinated attempt to blacken Bazoft's name in the cause of continued good relations with Iraq and that the details of his past emerged by accident.

What is certain, however, is that the Iraqis tried posthumously to blacken Bazoft's reputation by leaking a forged confession linking him to none other than Dr Gerald Bull, the inventor of the supergun. The confession, allegedly in Bazoft's handwriting, purported to show that he had been recruited by an employee of British and US intelligence to spy on Iraqi military facilities under journalistic cover. According to the 'confession', Bazoft's contact had told him that the plant at al-Hillah was important to Iraq's missile programme and that two Americans were employed at the site – Gerald Bull, its designer, and Steven Adams, a specialist in chemical weapons. The purpose of the plant, it was said, was to develop missiles which could deliver chemical warheads to Israel and Iran. The document also purported to show that Bazoft had met Bull and Adams in Cologne in 1988 and that on his illicit visit to al-Hillah he had been 'eager to catch Bull at the plant'. Bazoft's intelligence contact told him that if he caught the Americans 'he would get me a great amount of money'.

The alleged confession was leaked in April 1990, three weeks after Bazoft's execution. On 28 March, British customs had revealed an Iraqi attempt to smuggle American-made nuclear triggers via Britain and two weeks later seized a consignment of high precision steel piping produced by the British firm Sheffield Forgemasters. This was destined for Iraq where it was to be assembled into a supergun designed by Dr Bull. Until then the name of Dr Bull was unknown to the public and his murder, when he was shot in the head in Brussels on 22 March, had gone virtually unreported.

The Bazoft 'confession', however, appeared to link the executed journalist to a plot involving the CIA, British intelligence and possibly Israel, to undermine Dr Bull's work on Iraq's weapons' programme. It was a highly sophisticated operation; the document appeared to be in Bazoft's hand, although a graphologist later judged it to be a forgery. It was leaked together with what purported to be Bazoft's telex and telephone bill from the Ishtar Sheraton Hotel in Baghdad which showed that he made calls to the London office of Defence Systems Limited, a British company specializing in international security and headed by a former SAS officer, Alastair Morrison; the alleged confession had named Bazoft's intelligence contact as 'Morrison'. Mr Morrison, however, was to deny all knowledge of Bazoft. The journalist had stayed at the Meridien Hotel but was alleged to have made his calls from the business centre at the Ishtar and to have paid in cash; this appears to have been an attempt to show that Bazoft was covering his traces. The Iraqis also leaked a copy of a telex which appeared to show that $2,500 had been transferred to Bazoft from an unknown source during his stay in Baghdad.

The manner in which the Iraqis engineered the leak was as sophisticated as the documents themselves. Although the alleged confession had not been produced at Bazoft's trial, it formed part of a dossier presented by Saddam to Arab leaders to justify the journalist's execution. In addition, Saddam informed Prince Sultan, the Saudi defence minister, that Britain was involved in an intelligence operation based in Oman to spy on Saudi Arabia's newly acquired Chinese CS2 missiles. The result of these briefings was that the states of the Arab Gulf stood firmly behind Saddam in the row with the West over the execution.

The ironic postscript to the plot to discredit Bazoft was that the original tip-off – that Iraq might be in a position to provide new, inside information on the Bazoft affair – came from a Kuwaiti.

The Invasion

The supergun and nuclear trigger affairs, the outcry over the execution of Bazoft and the ceaseless press campaign over human rights left Saddam Hussein in no doubt that he was the victim of a Western-inspired plot to isolate and contain him. He resolved once more that attack was the best form of defence. In the spring of 1990, using the traditional method to win an Arab consensus in his favour, he threatened Israel, saying he would burn half the state with chemical weapons if he was attacked. Having established the ground rules, he then offered to host a summit of the Arab League in Baghdad, a move supported by Egypt but condemned by Syria as blackmail by the 'arrogant Iraqi regime'.

The emergency summit of the Arab League which opened in Baghdad on 28 May was sub-titled the 'Summit of Pan-Arab Security', a painful irony in the light of events in the Gulf later that summer. The pretext for the meeting was the threat posed by the mass immigration of Soviet Jews to Israel – 150,000 were expected to arrive that year. But Saddam, as host, had his own agenda, and this centred on his growing conflict with the West and his impending aggression in the Gulf.

Tareq Aziz, Saddam's foreign minister, had set the scene for the summit the previous month when he said that, in the light of threats facing the Arab world, 'there are some political, financial and, perhaps, military requirements which must be agreed upon by Arab leaders'. He added: 'We can't accept that we are dealt with as though we were accused of having no desire for peace simply because we make a scientific achievement or possess the kinds of weapons that enable us to defend ourselves against any attack.'

It was clear from the opening session that, in the name of confronting Israel and the West, Saddam intended to use the summit to legitimize his arms build-up and to pose as the natural protector of the Arab nation. He was also determined to taunt the United States and Britain in the wake of the 'supergun' and nuclear trigger affairs. Immediately before the summit, Washington had not only asked Egypt to try to inject a note of moderation, it had also appealed directly to Saddam to avoid ritual attacks on US imperialism. He declined to oblige, denouncing the United States as the main hostile force in the region because it continued to arm and finance Israel.

Saddam said an Israeli attack would not be possible without support from US imperialism. 'And I add the word "imperialism" because . . . I read the US State Department's note, which advised us against using the expression.'

The Baghdad summit defined the split which was to divide the Arab world after the invasion of Kuwait, and confirmed the emergence of a radical axis encompassing Iraq, Jordan and the PLO, opposed both to the moderation of Mubarak and the alleged parsimony of the conservative Gulf states. The Egyptian president's appeal to the summit to give an Arab message that was 'humane and rational, in line with the concepts of the age', went unheeded. King Hussein adopted the role of spokesman for his host, attacking the 'vicious and outrageous campaign' against Iraq launched by those who opposed Saddam's right to strategic parity with Israel. And he castigated the Gulf states for failing to provide the finances needed to combat the 'sinister plots' against his own kingdom. 'All that we ask is that you provide Jordan with the means to remain strong in order to buttress its economic and social security and to enhance its military power on its soil in order to withstand any onslaught until Arab military aid has arrived.' King Hussein was under the illusion, in May at least, that 'Arab military aid' – the Iraqi army – was intended to be used to counter Israeli aggression against Jordan rather than to mount an invasion in the Gulf.

Palestinian delegates privately expressed disillusion with the ability of American diplomacy to resolve the Arab–Israeli conflict and said that the best hope was for Iraq to achieve strategic parity with Israel. 'We believe that when Iraq builds itself up economically and militarily, it will create the material base for a balanced settlement of the Middle East crisis,' a PLO representative said. 'That's the main reason Iraq is threatened. Syria talked about gaining a strategic balance, but it's Iraq that did it. The main force of Israel is the atomic bomb and one has to remember that the strategic balance between the superpowers finally led to détente.' For the sake of peace, Iraq should be allowed to acquire the atomic bomb.

The radical rhetoric of Saddam and King Hussein drowned out the more moderate voices of Mubarak and his Gulf supporters and also overshadowed what was perhaps the most fundamental shift to emerge at the summit – Iraq's move towards a peace settlement with Iran. In his opening speech, Saddam dropped his customary attacks on Iran and spoke instead of an exchange of letters with President Ali Akbar Hashemi Rafsanjani 'which we hope will lead to direct and deep dialogue that would result in comprehensive peace'. In the two years since the Gulf war ended it was the first indication that the two sides were anywhere near negotiating a lasting peace.

Western diplomats who monitored the Summit proceedings regarded Saddam's intemperate language towards Israel as a bluff. The main long-term threat, according to the widely accepted analysis, still came from Iran. True, Iraq had announced in January that it had launched a satellite into space and its new Tammuz missile was said to have a range of 1,200 miles, but these developments were still in their infancy. A new squadron of Soviet SU24s had recently been delivered, but the air force, it was argued, still had a long way to go before it matched the Israelis'.

There was no doubt, however, that at the time of the Baghdad summit Saddam felt himself to be under intense pressure and probably genuinely feared that Israel, with US backing, was preparing to carry out a pre-emptive strike against his missile plants, just as it had destroyed the Osirak nuclear reactor in 1981. In the light of this perceived threat, he saw the apparent reluctance of the Gulf states to bend to his will as part of an all-encompassing conspiracy against Iraq. At the root of what he later called 'that black conspiracy spearheaded by the rulers of Kuwait against Iraq', Saddam saw an attempt to manipulate the oil market in order to keep down prices and starve Iraq of resources.

He gave the first hint of aggression against Kuwait when he said at that same summit meeting: 'War takes place sometimes through soldiers and damage is inflicted by explosives, killings or coup attempts. At other times, war is launched through economic means. To those who do not mean to wage war against Iraq, I say that this is a kind of war against Iraq.'

The dispute went on for months, but in July 1990 it came into the open. For the first time Iraq showed in public how angry it was at Kuwait and the Emirates, and how determined it was to put things right. The reasons were plain: Iraq was broke and unable to pay its debts, let alone rebuild its shattered economy. If this was the inevitable result of the war which Saddam himself had launched, that made no difference. The decision was taken to force Iraq's creditors to give up their claims, to see that those who had brought down the price of oil by over-production were made to stop, and to pick on super-rich Kuwait for quick help, which could be disguised as payment for oil 'stolen' from the Rumaileh field.

Saddam's plan to squeeze Kuwait may have been precipitated by the Kuwaiti policy of attempting to restore its relations with Iran, which had so deteriorated during the war that the Iranians had branded Kuwait at one time as a 'co-belligerent with Iraq'.

Iran and Kuwait quickly agreed to restore diplomatic relations, and on 11 July, three weeks before the invasion, the Iranian foreign minister, Ali Akbar Velayati, called in at Kuwait on his way home from acrimonious talks with his Iraqi counterpart in Geneva. It was a bad portent for Iraq, which feared that Kuwait might be seeking Iranian protection in the face of the spate of demands on it from Baghdad.

So on 16 July, Iraq wrote an open letter to the Arab League, something rarely done in the Arab world, where disputes between member states of the League are regarded as family matters, to be settled in private by Arab mediators. Not this time. Without mincing any words, Iraq accused Kuwait of 'stealing' $2.4 billion of oil by drilling into the Rumaileh field, which according to the Iraqis belonged to them, even though five kilometres at the southern tip is within Kuwaiti territory.

Iraq also accused Kuwait – with its 17,000-strong army compared to Iraq's million men under arms – of aggression against Baghdad. The grounds were that, without notice or consultation, Kuwait had moved the border and customs posts north from their previous positions; the Kuwaitis pointed out that both were still in Kuwaiti territory, and said if they had been moved, then it was for administrative and practical reasons, to expedite the flow of traffic.

Kuwait, never a country to be intimidated for all its lack of size or population, responded heatedly: it accused Iraq of resorting to intimidation to try to force it and other creditor countries into writing off Iraq's huge debts, something which the Kuwaitis strongly implied that they had no intention of doing. Two days later Iraq claimed Kuwait was preparing the ground for foreign intervention in the Gulf, and that it had renounced the Arab option in settling the dispute – a possibility that had not been mentioned until then. This was the signal for diplomats from a number of Arab countries to move in, and the Saudi Arabians, the Egyptians and Arab League officials all became involved. By 22 July Iraq was applying military as well as diplomatic pressure; the Americans, scrutinizing their satellite pictures, revealed that Iraq had moved 30,000 troops to the Kuwaiti border, and began to take a direct interest themselves.

The American State Department restated the standing policy: 'We remain determined to defend the principle of freedom of navigation and to ensure the free flow of oil through the Strait of Hormuz.' That was the formulation used during the Gulf war, when the United States sent its navy to protect Kuwaiti tankers from Iranian attack: it inevitably looked as though oil, not principle, was at the head of the American agenda. And with good cause: the United States in 1990 was more dependent than ever before on imported oil, at a historic high of 52 per cent, of which 11.5 per cent came from the Gulf. At the time of the first use of the oil weapon by the Arabs in 1973, the United States was importing 34.8 per cent of its needs, and by the time of the second oil shock in 1979, that figure had risen to 43.1 per cent.

The State Department formula indicated that self-interest was at work, and held no message for Iraq that the territorial integrity of small states was a concern. Then, realizing the reaction around the world, the State Department hastily added a rider: 'We also remain strongly committed to supporting the individual and collective self-defence of our friends in the Gulf, with whom we have deep and long-standing ties.' To underline that fact, the United States quickly arranged a joint military exercise with the United Arab Emirates, the first ever, and sent navy ships to patrol the northern Gulf.

Kuwait returned to the state of alert it had announced on 16 July and cancelled three days later. President Mubarak, due to host an Arab League meeting in Cairo in November, held talks with various foreign ministers in Cairo, then flew to Baghdad, Kuwait and Saudi Arabia for on-the-spot discussions. According to the Egyptian leader's account of his talks in Baghdad, Saddam Hussein said he had no intention of attacking Kuwait. Coupling this with his remarks to April Glaspie, the American ambassador, the world concluded that all Iraq's troop movements were mere sabre-rattling, that Saddam was only adopting bully-boy tactics to put pressure on Kuwait in advance of the OPEC meeting due in Geneva on 27 July. Washington officials congratulated themselves on having helped to defuse 'this brief mid-July crisis' by deploying a few planes and six warships, and no one looked at what had actually been said. A closer examination would have revealed that far from promising not to attack Kuwait, Saddam Hussein had said merely that he would take no action while negotiations went on.

Nor did he. Instead, he pursued to the full the advantage his rough tactics had given him. As the thirteen OPEC ministers assembled in Geneva, they were not merely looking over their shoulders, but also at the situation on the Iraq–Kuwait border. OPEC conferences were supposed to be quiet and gentlemanly affairs at which interests were balanced, guidelines set, and quotas agreed. In Geneva in 1990 it was not like that. As the delegates gathered in the unlovely surroundings of the Intercontinental Hotel, just up the road from the Palais des Nations which is one of the main European offshoots of the UN, all their attention was on the Gulf.

When the Iraqis arrived, led by the oil minister, Issam al-Shalabi, they immediately set the goal for the conference: a $25 a barrel benchmark price to replace the current $18. It seemed a wild idea at a time when there was a world glut of oil, when the northern summer further reduced demand, and cut across the known Saudi commitment to a 'reasonable' price in order to maintain a balance between production costs and the related prices of goods the oil states had to import from the manufacturing countries.

It was also remembered that only months before the price had been $14, and that at its worst, from the producers' point of view, it had gone as low as $8. Yet the Iraqis bowled in with their $25 demand, quickly backed by the opportunists in the Libyan delegation, and no one seemed unduly alarmed.

On the second morning, the fruits of what in Geneva are called 'bilaterals' began to show up – the results of all those late-night meetings in smoky rooms with bottles of Black Label. Iran stepped in with a suggested compromise benchmark price of $23; Iraq appeared reluctant, but would clearly have gone along with that; Venezuela bowed out and made plain it had only been talking for its mentor Saudi Arabia; Nigeria and others abandoned any attempt to play a role, and the Saudis reminded everyone that they could and would swing the markets if necessary, either by discounting or by increasing production.

An hour of tough talking in an eighth-floor suite by Hisham Nazer of Saudi Arabia, Shalabi for Iraq, and Gholamreza Agazadeh for Iran in the presence of Sheikh Rashid Salim al-Amiri of Kuwait, and it was all over; the delegates solemnly trooped back to the first floor for a final plenary session at which the benchmark price was fixed at $21 – the maximum that Saudi Arabia would accept.

Shalabi, for Iraq, said he was very happy with the outcome, and added that his country had no intention of enforcing quota discipline: 'I have no police uniform. We do not want to act as policemen.'

Nonetheless, a second part of the agreement called for production to be limited to 22.5 million barrels a day, and there was no doubt this time that if the quota-busters tried their usual tricks, they would be in trouble. There was also a small sub-clause stating that any future increase in production would be linked to a rise in prices, which again pleased those in favour of benefiting the producers at the expense of the consumers. It was all a splendid compromise, everyone agreed, as the champagne was opened in the private suites, and perhaps it had been no bad thing that Saddam Hussein had acted tough; after all, someone had to impose discipline...

The only trouble was that having achieved its purpose, the Iraqi troops showed no signs of being dispersed. As everyone began moving back from the crisis, it was left to lorry-drivers and travellers coming from Basra to Kuwait to report that far from moving out, the Iraqi army was moving in. They said there were long hold-ups because columns of tanks and artillery were driving south, that tented camps had been struck because troops were in trucks heading south, and that there was no sign of the Iraqis going back home.

To make it all worse, Iraq announced the postponement of talks with Kuwait which were to have taken place in Jeddah to resolve all the outstanding contentious issues between them. Even reports that by this stage Iraq had 100,000 troops on the border failed to alert the international community; after all, Iraq had already shown it was prepared to use the threat of force to pursue its commercial interests, so no doubt it was doing the same in preparation for the meeting between Izzat Ibrahim, the Iraqi number two, and Prince Saad, the Kuwaiti prime minister, which would eventually take place in Jeddah on 1 August.

But nothing happened at those talks. The Iraqi side approached them in much the same way they had begun negotiations with Iran at the end of the Gulf war – as a victor dictating terms to a defeated enemy. Kuwait did not look at it like that; it saw the meeting as the opening of negotiations which might be tough, but which would eventually be resolved. On the eve of the Jeddah meeting, Prince Saad said; 'I am looking forward with open heart to the meeting with my brother Izzat Ibrahim, the leader of the Iraqi delegation. This is a passing crisis.'

But at that first meeting Prince Saad stated there could be no question of territorial concessions, nor any admission that Kuwait had 'stolen' oil for which it had to pay. On the question of Iraq's debt to Kuwait, there was room for negotiation, he said. It was Kuwait's opening bid in a process which the emirate assumed would be the usual haggle, and which would end up with both sides making compromises and finally reaching a position which both could accept.

The Iraqis did not see it like that. Izzat Ibrahim, a Saddam loyalist raised from poverty and now related to the president by marriage, believed he was there to collect the spoils of victory. In any event, he had no mandate to negotiate; only Saddam could do that. Izzat was sent to give a message, to set down the terms on which Iraq was prepared to allow Kuwait to continue an independent existence – under Iraqi domination, of course. Anything less than total acceptance was defiance. So after one meeting the Iraqi delegation went back to Baghdad.

In what was initially seen as giving the screw just one more turn, Iraq closed the land border between the two countries. Twelve hours later, the Iraqi invasion began. As usual, Saddam Hussein had been setting out his intentions, not putting forward his negotiating terms.

And so the talking stopped, and the brief war began. The West and Egypt could only acknowledge an intelligence disaster. In Washington, attempts to find scapegoats who had 'lost Kuwait' were countered by unsourced claims that the CIA had predicted what would happen all along. In Britain, with its historic links with the region, there was, at least, no attempt to cover up; the experts, it was privately acknowledged, had simply got it wrong. An assessment made available to British ministers by the Cabinet Office the day before the invasion concluded that Iraq would not invade.

Saddam later claimed that his statements over the previous ten weeks had provided adequate warning of his intentions, and in so doing had given an opportunity for Kuwait to mend its ways. 'Does not all this constitute warnings made in advance, but in vain?' he said in a message to the American people. 'Was there not a provocation, indeed a flagrant aggression, against Iraq? Is not all this evidence enough for understanding the measures we took on and after 2 August 1990?'

When the Iraqi tanks rolled across the border into Kuwait at 2 a.m. on 2 August, only two squadrons were ready to fight. Those 24 tanks had their full complement of armour-piercing and fragmentation shells, machine gun ammunition, spares and fuel; all the rest carried the minimum, and some had no ammunition at all. The result was that the lightly laden tanks could sweep down on Kuwait city at 50 mph, leaving the fighting armoured vehicles to take out any opposition encountered; none was. As expected, the Kuwaiti armed forces put up no resistance at all at the border, and it was only when the Iraqis reached Kuwait that a few gallant defenders tried to stop them, with disastrous consequences. Nor did the Kuwait air force or navy play any part. The best pilots in the air force (and there were not many) did go to the air base and fly their planes – but with discretion if not gallantry, headed south to Saudi Arabia, ready to fight another day.

The tiny navy was not involved at all. The 20-odd patrol boats which were all the navy could boast were used to protect Kuwait from smugglers, and particularly from the Iraqi dhows which occasionally attempted to land a valuable cargo of alcoholic drinks in the dry emirate. Even this was something more than a dutiful upholding of the ban on alcohol; drink of various kinds was always available, but the smuggling monopoly was in the hands of a few minor princes of the Sabah family who wanted no competition from outsiders who might be ready to take a smaller margin of profit. So the navy stayed in port, the air force flew away, and the army barely managed a token resistance; everything went just as the Iraqis had planned.

The only thing that went wrong was that the emir and all his ministers managed to escape. The Iraqi contingency plan called for the emir to be captured or killed, so Republican Guards headed straight for the Dasman Palace as soon as they got to Kuwait, planning to offer the ruler a choice: if he agreed to 'co-operate', to order an end to all resistance, and to stay on as head of a quisling government which would be directed from Baghdad, he would be allowed to live. If, as expected, the emir refused the offers made to him, he would be shot in his palace, resisting the overtures of the friendly Iraqi forces.

It never came to that. In the few hours which were all it took for the Iraqis to reach the city, the duty officers at defence headquarters had managed to alert the government; the minister of defence, Sheikh Nawaf, hurried to the command post, was given an account of what was going on, and as he told us later in Saudi Arabia, sensibly left the soldiers to cope while he hurried off to warn the other ministers and the emir. By the time the Iraqis reached the Dasman Palace, the emir was well on his way to the Saudi border, and the only senior figure left who stayed behind with the palace guards was Sheikh Fahd, the emir's brother, known around the world as the manager of the very good Kuwaiti football team.

Sheikh Fahd was the one hero of the whole affair. He stood with a few guards at the top of the palace steps as the first Iraqis arrived, barring their way with drawn pistol. One of the Iraqis casually shot him dead.

A few weeks later, at the new seat of the Kuwaiti government in the Saudi summer capital at Taif, the al-Hada Sheraton, the ministers described to us their actions on the night of the invasion, and their escapes. There were no tales of heroism; not a single minister even glimpsed an Iraqi soldier, or came close to what fighting there was. They seemed to have spent the night talking to each other on the telephone or scurrying about in their cars – still telephoning as the chauffeurs took them around the city – and eventually speeding off south. Some stopped to spend the day at their beach houses before forming new ministerial convoys to head off to Saudi Arabia.

In Kuwait city there were many individual acts of bravery, and a few units put up spirited resistance before being mown down by the ruthless firepower of the Iraqis. But in seven hours it was all over; Kuwait was totally invested by the invaders, the government gone, armed resistance at an end, and the airport closed. An unfortunate British Airways plane en route to India landed in Kuwait just as the invasion began: the crew and passengers were taken prisoner, and the men moved to Baghdad to form part of the human shield which Saddam so quickly deployed to protect vital targets. It was the sort of quick and efficient victory he had tried for in vain against Iran.

But Saddam had misread the West as much as it had misread him, and despite the warnings he had himself given, he did not appreciate the extent of the new superpower relationship. On the day of the invasion the UN Security Council met and approved Resolution 660, condemning the aggression and calling for Iraq's immediate withdrawal. Responding to appeals from the Kuwaitis for international assistance, President Bush ordered additional US warships to the Gulf and Moscow halted the flow of Soviet weapons to Iraq. Kuwait's ambassador to the UN, Sheikh Saud Nasir al-Sabah, told the White House: 'We would like to have military assistance in order to survive. I think US intervention at this stage is of paramount importance.'

The main banking centres put a freeze on Kuwaiti assets, thereby depriving Saddam of his booty and, within a day, the Russians and the Americans had condemned the invasion in a joint statement issued in Moscow by the Soviet foreign minister Eduard Shevardnadze and the visiting US secretary of state, James Baker. Within twenty-four hours a collective international response, which Saddam had discounted, was already emerging.

Saddam initially claimed that Iraqi troops had entered Kuwait at the request of a revolutionary movement opposed to the al-Sabah, but this claim was soon discredited by his inability to find Kuwaiti nationals willing to serve in a puppet government. This did not prevent the Iraqis installing a provisional cabinet on 4 August which three days later declared Kuwait a republic. The head of this short-lived regime was Alaa Hussein Ali, said to be a colonel in the Kuwaiti army. Kuwaiti sources, however, identified Alaa as an Iraqi officer who had fought in the Gulf war and written a military history of the conflict and who, until the invasion, had been in charge of Iraq's Fao-1 anti-missile missile programme.

The US's immediate concern was to prevent any Iraqi incursion into Saudi Arabia. President Bush stressed that 'the integrity of Saudi Arabia, its freedom, are very, very important to us,' and he promised US support to repel any Iraqi attack. On 6 August the US defence secretary, Richard Cheney, was in Jeddah to discuss contingency plans, and on the same day, the Security Council stepped up the pressure by passing Resolution 661, imposing mandatory trade sanctions which included a ban on Iraqi and Kuwaiti oil, a measure which had already been adopted by the West.

That same day, the American chargé d'affaires in Baghdad, Joseph Wilson, was called in to see Saddam. This was the first opportunity since the invasion for the United States to judge Saddam's intentions directly and so Wilson's preoccupation was to secure guarantees for the security of Saudi Arabia. Saddam summed up for Wilson the Iraqi arguments in support of the invasion and of Iraq's 'special relationship' with Kuwait, before warning the United States against interfering in Gulf affairs or in the 'brotherly' relations between Iraq and Saudi Arabia. 'Not only did the good relationship between Iraq and Saudi Arabia not cause harm to the United States, it was one of the factors of stability in the area. So meddling in the relations between Iraq and Saudi Arabia will destabilize the area and cause harm to US interests . . . We were brothers, but you spoiled that relationship between us and you turned the Saudis against us.'

He clearly believed the pressure against him in the first half of 1990 related purely to the threat he posed to Israel, and from this he drew the conclusion that he was free to act with impunity in the Gulf. He told Wilson that he believed certain Western and US circles had been advising Israel to attack Iraq, and he defended his verbal attacks on Israel as an act of peace. 'We believe that helped peace instead of keeping silent and letting Israel attack us and then counter-attacking.'

When asked by Wilson for an assurance that Iraq had no intention of undertaking any military action against Saudi Arabia, Saddam replied: 'You can take that assurance to the Saudis. We will not attack those who do not attack us, we will not harm those who do not harm us. Those who want our friendship will find us more than eager to be friendly. As for Saudi Arabia, that question did not even occur in my mind.'

Neither Bush nor King Fahd were comforted by Saddam's assurances and on 7 August the US president announced in a televised address to the nation that the 82nd Airborne Division was being dispatched to Saudi Arabia; it was the start of Operation Desert Shield, the largest deployment of American troops overseas since the Vietnam war. Bush was uncompromising; he accused Saddam of an 'outrageous and brutal act of aggression' and indirectly compared him to Hitler: 'Appeasement does not work,' he said. 'As was the case in the 1930s, we see in Saddam Hussein an aggressive dictator threatening his neighbours . . .'

Bush also listed his four guiding principles: immediate and unconditional withdrawal of all Iraqi forces from Kuwait, the restoration of the legitimate Kuwaiti government, a reaffirmation of the US commitment to stability in the Gulf, and America's determination to protect the lives of its citizens.

Saddam's response the following day was to proclaim the annexation of Kuwait, the first annexation of a sovereign state since the Second World War. The announcement of 'a comprehensive and eternal merger' was, on the face of it, a grave tactical error which turned international opinion against Iraq. Even Saddam's putative allies in the Security Council, Cuba and Yemen, found it hard to defend him.

Saddam would have liked to portray himself as the victim of an Anglo–American conspiracy, but now faced the active opposition of a wide range of states. Egypt had already promised troops for a multinational force and now Syria, Morocco, Pakistan and Bangladesh followed suit, joining Saudi Arabia and the Gulf states. The encirclement of Iraq had begun. Turkey, which had already closed the Iraqi pipeline which crossed its territory, gave permission for twenty-eight American F111 long-range fighter-bombers to be transferred from Britain to its Nato bases, and began to move its own troops down to the Iraqi border.

At the start of the crisis Margaret Thatcher was in the United

States, where she had gone for talks with Bush and to receive an award from the Aspen Institute in Colorado. British officials did little to counter subsequent speculation that it was she who was responsible for encouraging Bush's tough line against the invasion.

Thatcher certainly took a firm line in her Aspen speech, saying the invasion 'defies every principle for which the UN stands', adding: 'If we let it succeed no small country can ever feel safe again. The law of the jungle takes over.' But she seemed content to let Bush take the lead in handling the crisis and was at first uncharacteristically reluctant to become directly involved in co-ordinating the British response, leaving the task to her ministers.

The Western response was complicated by Iraq's refusal to provide exit visas for the several thousand Westerners in Kuwait and Iraq. Saddam called them 'guests' and 'heroes of peace', but by any normal standard they were hostages, particularly when they were moved to strategic sites which were likely targets of US bombing. No Western politician actually described the hostages as expendable, of course, but this was the underlying sentiment on the Western side. Bush had seen President Carter's presidency destroyed by the Iranian hostage crisis of 1979–81 in which the lives of the fifty-two Americans held in Iran had been placed above all other considerations.

Although Saddam Hussein was rarely seen on television after the invasion, he did attempt to make use of the medium once he had openly committed himself to using foreigners as hostages. On 19 August, in a message read out on his behalf, Saddam put an end to this pretence. Ostensibly directed to the families of those being held, the message said President Bush would have to give an unequivocal written promise to pull American forces out of the Gulf before Iraq would allow the foreigners to leave. The American promise would have to be backed by a Security Council guarantee that the troops deployed would leave according to a fixed timetable which should be no longer than the time taken to send them there in the first place.

The Iraqi ambassador in Paris, Abdul Razzaq al-Hashemi, said Westerners had been housed at potential targets from the north to the south of Iraq. He echoed the warning given by Saadi Mehdi Saleh, the speaker of Iraq's puppet National Assembly: foreigners would be treated according to the way in which their countries acted towards Iraq and the diligence with which they imposed sanctions. Some Austrian, Swedish, Finnish and Portuguese, for instance, were allowed to go immediately because their governments had not joined in the military build-up in Saudi Arabia.

A few days later Saddam Hussein mounted the bizarre television spectacle which, more than anything else, united public opinion all over the world against his use of civilians as a human shield. Saddam Hussein chose a group of British people, including two young boys, to explain through an interpreter what he was doing and why; he said he sympathized with them and understood that they would rather be back in their homes, but explained that he was trying to avoid 'the scourge of war'. The interpreter told the group of fifteen men, women and children: 'Saddam Hussein would like it to be known the role he played in maintaining peace, and in preventing a war. You will all be heroes for maintaining peace.'

Patting seven-year-old Stuart Lockwood on the head, and bringing an eleven-year-old boy forward to stand next to him, Saddam played on the nerves of everyone with a relative in Iraq or Kuwait – and there were many of them. Britain had at least 4,000 people in Kuwait alone, the United States 2,500, and there were contingents from all European countries.

Saddam no doubt had in mind the Iranians' successful manipulation of their hostages ten years earlier. But, not for the first time, he miscalculated; instead of causing public pressure for governments to negotiate, there was a public outcry of disgust at this blatant use of children, old men and women. Such was the condemnation that Saddam changed his policy, and on 29 August announced that all women and children would be released, although the men would still be held at the various centres around the country. Over the months, Saddam continued to use the hostages to try to put pressure on America and its allies, releasing a few now and then as distinguished former ministers – Willy Brandt, Ted Heath, Bulent Ecevit, Tony Benn – made the pilgrimage to

Baghdad to seek freedom for their countrymen.

Within days of the invasion the two or three million Arabs, Indians, Pakistanis and Far Eastern nationals who had provided Kuwait's manual labour began to flee the potential war zone. In three months, three-quarters of a million people passed through Jordan alone, with another 250,000 finding their way out through Turkey, Iran or Syria. The situation in Jordan was at first chaotic, and there were terrible conditions in the camps at Ruweishid on the border. But voluntary organizations and UN agencies moved in to help Jordan, and the refugees were sent on their way within a reasonable time.

The worst effect was on the Jordanian government and people: because Jordan had failed to side with the West, and King Hussein was the most active and persuasive apologist for Iraq, there was little support from Western governments in alleviating the huge burden on Jordan's scant resources; nor was there any help for the Jordanian people, who found themselves going short because of the needs of the refugees, while prices soared.

We saw one of the more curious effects of Saddam's hostage policy during the months of diplomatic wrangling as the alliance brought pressure on the regime. Confronted with obvious Westerners walking freely about Baghdad, taxi drivers and shopkeepers would make a guess at the nationality: 'Yugoslav?' they would ask, as many workers from that country stayed at their jobs in the oil industry and construction sectors until there was no more work to do. 'Irish?' was sometimes the question, as doctors and both male and female nurses and technicians stayed on at the Irish-run Parc Hospital — when their contracts ended they were refused permits to leave, but instead offered new employment. Few of them took new contracts, holding on in the hope of an exit visa, although a number of them worked voluntarily for something to do.

There were many foreigners going about their normal business: workmen from Portugal, Belgium and Britain at Saddam Hussein's vast and ornate new palace in Baghdad, diplomats based in the capital who were able to move freely, and the 8,000 or so

Soviet experts and their families who had been working with the armed forces or in the oil industry.

But in general, people tried not to go about too much; there was never any trouble, but there was a slightly uncomfortable feeling. At the airport, an Iraqi who had worked for years in Britain asked us: 'Why aren't you being held? Why are they letting you out?' Told we were journalists, he immediately became charming and helpful; the Iraqi policy of making propaganda ran deep.

In Kuwait, hundreds of people of various nationalities stayed hidden for months, held until their release at the end of 1990. If they were found, they were picked up by the Iraqis and taken to Baghdad to add to the human shield, but many remained, often living in the houses of friendly Kuwaitis. The American, French and British embassies remained staffed the longest of all – the British ambassador did the cooking and the consul the washing up – as governments sought to maintain a symbolic presence as a means of denying the legitimacy of the Iraqi occupation.

Although the journalists who visited Baghdad were not harassed, the Americans in particular were always nervous, and carefully avoided any actions which might make them liable to Iraqi law, such as changing money on the black market. This made life difficult because the Iraqi dinar, officially worth $3, had gone to three dinars to the dollar within days of the invasion of Kuwait, and later was selling at as much as ten dinars to the dollar.

The press corps too had other reasons for unhappiness. Everyone was concentrated into one hotel, the unattractive Rashid, a little way out from the centre of town instead of on the main Saadoun Street. The Rashid was built to house visiting heads of state and official delegations, so it is surrounded by a high wall with block towers at the corners, and has heavy wrought-iron gates which are electronically controlled. As many noted, the place could have been sealed in minutes.

Within days of the imposition of sanctions, all restaurants in Baghdad and other cities were ordered to close. The order was rescinded, then reimposed on the up-market places only, leaving the press to eat in small hole-in-the-wall coffee houses.

There were also fears early on – not just among the press – that the brewery in Baghdad would have to close down through lack of sugar. Fortunately the government realized that was the one thing which might have caused riots in the streets, and quickly ensured supplies. The Iraqis, alone among Arabs, are a nation of drinkers – their national poet, Abu Nawas, is shown with a wine-cup in his hand in the gardens beside the Tigris. Along Saadoun street and in some of the small beer bars around Rashid Street, every evening Iraqis would get through huge numbers of bottles of beer – though all this consumption rarely seemed to make them talkative.

The embargo had few visible effects in the city, though many industrial plants had to close down for lack of spares and the generating station ran at only 25 per cent capacity.

Joseph Wilson, the American chargé, visited the Iraqi foreign office most days, and told us his greatest problem was to convince the Iraqis that President Bush was serious, that there was a real danger of war. General Michael Dugan succeeded where the diplomat failed: in an unguarded interview which was published, the general, the commander of the US air force, said if hostilities began, he would bomb downtown Baghdad, Saddam Hussein, his bodyguards and his mistress. Cheney, the defence secretary, promptly sacked Dugan, a move which reinforced the Iraqi belief that he was speaking the truth. This was confirmed for Iraq when Dugan was immediately given a new job as an adviser, and allowed to stay on past retiring age.

For ordinary Iraqis, the first difficulty caused by the embargo was finding bread. Like all Arabs, the Iraqis insist on fresh bread daily, often at every meal, and think nothing of wasting large amounts. Within a month of the invasion, Iraq was harvesting a record grain crop, but in the earlier weeks it was very short of flour, and so quickly rationed bread. Until then, the situation was chaotic as each member of a family toured a neighbourhood joining the queues at different bakeries. Once rationing was introduced, waiting time was cut to a minimum and fair distribution ensured. After eight years of war, the Iraqi bureaucracy was expert at such things. But the bread produced contained more bran than wheat, and the Iraqis hated it.

It was not long before luxury goods unknown to Iraq appeared in the Baghdad shops and it became obvious that Kuwait was being looted. Often these still carried the marks of Kuwaiti stores, and no one made any pretence that they were locally produced or imported. Such items were freely available, but scarce commodities such as powdered milk – Iraq has no dairy industry – were rationed, with additional amounts only for those who could pay the high prices demanded. And within days of Saddam Hussein's speech giving Iran everything it had wanted from the Gulf war, Iranian goods began appearing in the shops. Even before this, we had seen an Iranian refrigerated container lorry from which boxes of eggs were being sold in a Baghdad street. Iranian officials, while promising that they would continue to apply sanctions in spite of Iraq's concessions, always noted that Iran had a 700-mile border with Iraq, that there was a long history of smuggling, and that Iranians were notable entrepreneurs.

Deals were done between Kurdish tribes on both sides of the border; the Iraqi Kurds bought whole flocks of sheep and goats from their kinsmen on the Iranian side, and paid with gold provided by the Iraqi Central Bank. In the north, the Kurds also did good business with Turkey, and the Iraqi army even built a new 15-mile road up to the border to facilitate smuggling.

Jordan, too, played its part: it was the one country to which Iraqi Airways flew twice a day, and it was noticeable that on the Baghdad–Amman leg all seats were occupied, but returning to Baghdad from Jordan the front compartment was left empty; clearly, there were weighty packages in the forward hold.

The long road from Amman across the desert through Ruweishid to Baghdad was also used, though more for propaganda purposes than to supply goods. The Jordanian Red Crescent organized convoys of lorries to take gifts of milk and medicines 'from the children of the stones (Palestinians) to the children of Iraq'. On several nights we saw lorry-loads of flour going across the border, and some of the truck-loads of food ostensibly heading for the refugee camps at Ruweishid may have gone further. In return, Jordan received oil at the rate of 33,000 barrels a day, though it was being sold at the discounted price of $16 a barrel, and most was in payment of debts.

King Hussein was in an impossible position; he had supported Iraq wholeheartedly during the Gulf war, recognizing that it would be good for his kingdom and would also fit in with the majority Arab view, something with which he always tried to identify. In the decade from 1980 he got to know Saddam well, and found, somewhat to his surprise, that he had come to like and admire him. Saddam, in the king's eyes, was a dedicated nationalist, a strong man beholden to no one, a genuine champion of Arabism.

With the invasion of Kuwait, the king found himself in difficulties: he realized such aggression could not be allowed, and publicly condemned it. But at least 70 per cent of his people, the Palestinians, applauded Saddam's defiance of America and at first shed no tears over the fate of the Sabahs; later, in the West Bank, we found Palestinians who ruefully admitted they had not realized how much PLO money came from Kuwait; it was only when the subsidies to the West Bank began to dry up that it dawned on them.

In Jordan, posters of Saddam, or of Saddam and the king, were displayed everywhere. There was no doubt where the sympathies of the majority of the people lay, and if the king had tried to disregard them, his throne would have been shakier than ever. As it was, his personal preference coincided with those of his people, though as an arch-survivor he was unhappy at having to argue with his friends and backers in the West – after all, the CIA had always given the king a personal contribution of $50 million a year 'to ensure the stability of the regime'.

Kuwait and the Gulf

The Kuwait invaded by Iraq on 2 August was a state in transition. Having successfully weathered serious internal upsets and external crises in its twenty-nine-year independent history, it was now taking steps to restore a form of parliamentary democracy which had twice been tried, and twice abandoned.

In Arab terms, it was one of the most open and tolerant countries of the region, with a lively press, a flourishing though unofficial political life, vast prosperity, reasonable emancipation for women, and a respected international diplomatic role. What it lacked at this time was the National Assembly which had once given Kuwait citizens a say in running the affairs of the state, and which had been suppressed by the emir because of the outspokenness of many of the deputies in criticizing the ruling family.

Throughout 1989, with the Gulf war over, former members of the assembly waged an effective campaign in Kuwait to win permission for new elections to be held, and for their country's parliament to be given new and wider powers; the campaign was resisted by the emir and his ministers, but was one to which they had been forced to bow shortly before the Iraqis made all such matters academic.

The means of bringing pressure on the rulers in Kuwait was a peculiarly local phenomenon, the system of 'diwaniya'. As in many Arab countries, local leaders held meetings, variously called majlis or diwaniya, at which their supporters could present petitions, discuss local and international affairs, or merely exchange news and views. In Kuwait, the system of diwaniya had been adapted for particular political purposes. On one day a week, usually a Tuesday, all the deposed politicians of the old National Assembly would host such conferences in the various districts of Kuwait city and in other towns. The meetings were well advertised in advance, so that as the campaign built up during the year, sometimes 2,000 or 3,000 people would turn up at the homes of the leading figures, Dr Ahmed al-Khatib, the leader of the nationalist faction, or the former speaker, Dr Ahmed Sa'adoun. Loudspeaker systems were rigged up so that the proceedings in the homes of these politicians, which could accommodate no more than a few dozen people, could be relayed to those outside.

As the meetings grew larger so the government and the police became more concerned, and eventually force was used to try to disperse the crowds and prevent meetings being held – with the predictable result that next time a diwaniya was called, even more people turned up.

In the end, the government had to give in, and in June of 1990, elections were authorized for a seventy-five member National Assembly of which one-third were to be the emir's appointments. The opposition refused this condition and boycotted the elections.

These tentative steps towards restoring democracy were abruptly brought to a halt by the invasion. Opposition leaders in Kuwait could have used this opportunity to take for themselves the sort of power they could never achieve under the continued rule of the al-Sabah, no matter how many new liberties were given to a reconstituted National Assembly. The Iraqis were desperate to find men of repute to act for them, to form a government and give some appearance of credibility to the Iraqi story that a group of 'young revolutionaries' had staged a revolt in Kuwait and called on Iraq to come to their aid.

Yet not a single member of the Kuwait opposition agreed to take part in such a charade. Despite intense pressure, every known opponent of the al-Sabah, everyone who had campaigned for so long to bring a measure of democracy to the state, refused to have anything to do with the invaders.

Instead, the opposition joined the al-Sabah in condemning the Iraqi invasion and agreed to put off until later their political ambitions. That those ambitions were still present was shown in a tough meeting in Taif in Saudi Arabia on 15 October when all sectors of the Kuwaiti public declared their determination to restore the sovereignty of their country. Some 700 representatives of different groups travelled to the Saudi resort for a meeting with the emir and the crown prince, including all the leading opponents of the autocratic style of rule of the al-Sabah, but without exception they put liberation before reform – though still emphasizing that reform would have to come once the Iraqis were driven out.

After some hesitation, Sheikh Saad accepted the conditions put by those present: 'National unity will be the groundwork on which to build our future Kuwait,' he said. 'The people of Kuwait can only be rewarded for their trust and loyalty by further trust.'

From this it was a small step to a pledge that once the situation was restored, there would be a return to the original 1962 constitution. Not only would there be a return to that constitution, with its inclusion of a fifty-member assembly, freedom of the press and the right of assembly, Sheikh Saad said, there would also be new rights for women, who had been barred from political life, even though they had more personal freedom than those in most countries of the Arabian peninsula – Kuwaiti women were even then amazing their Saudi Arabian sisters by their tales of driving their own cars, going unveiled if they chose, and taking a full part in business and professional life.

In return for the promises made by the crown prince, the groups who travelled to Taif agreed that once the Iraqis were forced out of Kuwait, the emir should be restored, with the crown prince. This undercut those who had been speaking of some compromise which would leave the al-Sabah out in deference to Saddam Hussein's repeated assertion that he would never allow the Kuwaiti ruler to be restored. Nor was there any talk of a referendum, as had been suggested by a number of the more radical Arab states such as Yemen and Libya.

It was presumably in part a response to the absence of collaborators that Saddam went ahead with annexation and the appointment of a civilian administrator to run the new nineteenth province of Iraq. For the first three months of the occupation this task fell to his cousin, the local government minister Ali Hassan al-Majid, a former head of security. Majid had been in charge of the 'Arabization' of Iraqi Kurdistan at the end of the Gulf war and had authorized the use of poison gas against the Pesh Merga and other dissidents; he extended the system of forced removal of Kurds from the border villages, and he authorized the army to subdue unrest. The result was that something like 100,000 Kurds fled from Iraq into Turkey and Iran.

A policy rather less brutal but with the same objectives was introduced in Kuwait. Within days of his appointment Majid ordered the border between Kuwait and Saudi Arabia to be opened, so that thousands of Kuwaitis could leave the country; only when they got to the border did they find that their Kuwaiti papers were to be taken away from them which meant that in future they might not be able to reclaim land or possessions in the emirate. Men between the ages of eighteen and forty-five were not allowed to leave, although their families were; the implication was that Kuwaiti men would have to do their military service in the Iraqi forces.

According to the Kuwaiti government and its followers based in Taif, there was a determined opposition to the Iraqis, with constant tales of Iraqi army vehicles being ambushed and set alight, Iraqi soldiers seized and stray officers killed. Certainly there was some opposition to the invaders, but it was minimal, ill-organized and fragmented. Some former members of the Kuwaiti armed forces and police attempted opposition, but they were up against a well-organized occupying force which did not hesitate to strike back hard. The stories of heroic Kuwaiti acts of martyrdom in the early days of the invasion owed more to propaganda than fact.

As an Iraqi official in Baghdad said at the time: 'If an Iraqi soldier on his own wandered down certain streets in Kuwait after dark, he might well be assaulted. On the other hand, Iraqi soldiers always carried their guns with them, and retribution was quick if anything did happen, with the result that after the first few days, there were very few incidents indeed.'

The fact was that the Kuwaitis had never expected to be invaded, and so had made no preparations for such an eventuality – not because they did not appreciate the threat from Iraq, but because they believed that any renewal of that threat would be bought off, just as previous Iraqi attempts to take over the emirate had been stopped.

There was nothing new about Iraq's claim on Kuwait: six days after Kuwait became independent on 19 June, 1961, Iraq declared that it considered Kuwait an indivisible part of Iraq, and that it would not recognize the independence agreement between London and Kuwait.

General Abdel Karim Qassem, the Iraqi president, spelt out his country's claim to Kuwait: the emirate was part of the former Ottoman vilayet of Basra, and Iraq was the successor to the Ottoman Empire. He said Kuwait's claim to independence amounted to mutiny and its purported agreement with Britain was meaningless.

> We shall extend Iraq's borders to the south of Kuwait. Iraq and nobody else concludes agreements about Kuwait, so we regard this agreement between Kuwait and Britain as illegal from the date of its operation. No individual, whether in Kuwait or outside, has the right to dominate the people of Kuwait, for they are the people of Iraq. The era of sheikhdoms is over. The people of Kuwait are still groaning under the oppression of British imperialism. One gigantic step will uproot imperialism from the earth and drive away its shadow.

Qassem's stand prompted a message of support from an unlikely source in the form of a telegram from Cairo, signed by his former would-be assassin, Saddam Hussein.

Despite the apparent belligerence of Qassem's remarks, they provoked little real concern, as there were no specific threats of annexation or invasion. Everyone accepted that the borders between Iraq and Kuwait, like the borders with Saudi Arabia, were ill-defined, if they were marked at all. They owed their origins to a remarkable conference called in 1922 by Sir Percy Cox, the British high commissioner in Baghdad.

Cox, one of the most influential and far-sighted Britons ever to serve in the Gulf, was coming to the end of his career; he had put Faisal on the throne in Iraq, but feared that the lawlessness on the country's southern border might threaten the stability of the new monarchy. To put an end to the troubles he summoned Ibn Saud, the ruler of Saudi Arabia, to a conference at Uqair, a small town on the Gulf opposite Bahrain. Cox wanted to define the northern borders of Saudi Arabia and to stop any further incursions by the king's marauding bedouin followers, who cared little for artificial frontiers but whose presence might later serve as a pretext for claims to sovereignty.

As the meetings and the quarrels continued, Cox decided to take the law into his own hands. In the course of one day he imposed a solution which, although it settled things at the time, left scope for endless trouble later on, perhaps culminating in the events of 1990. Taking a red pencil firmly in his hand, Sir Percy drew a line from the head of the Gulf to the frontier with Trans-Jordan, and then two more lines to create the 'neutral zones', areas which were to be shared among Saudi Arabia, Kuwait and Iraq. The map he was working on had little in the way of detail, the points he chose to start his lines were arbitrary, and not even geographically identifiable. His scheme satisfied no one, for it gave some Kuwaiti territory to Saudi Arabai, and Saudi land to the Iraqis, while the two neutral zones became the source of interminable arguments and feuds. Yet the decisions he made in Uqair in 1922 lasted for forty-five years.

At the time of Kuwaiti independence the borders between the emirate and Iraq, and those with Saudi Arabia, had not been defined any more precisely than by Sir Percy Cox's lines on an out-of-date map. So General Qassem's remarks just after Kuwait's independence were seen at first as no more than a reasonable restatement of his country's position at a time of change; no one was too perturbed, though Britain said it would be ready to receive any request for assistance from the ruler of Kuwait, as required under the new Treaty of Friendship between the two countries. Saudi Arabia and Iran both said they backed Kuwait, and the Arab

League offered to mediate and to use its good offices. It all appeared fairly unimportant.

Sheikh Abdullah al-Sabah, the Kuwaiti ruler, at first seemed to share this lack of concern. Then, just a week after making plain that he did not take the Iraqi claim seriously, he appealed to Britain for help. And, rather like the Americans in Saudi Arabia in 1990, the initiative came more from the would-be donor than from the recipient of the aid. On 3 July 1961, British forces began arriving in Kuwait; HMS *Bulwark* lay off-shore with helicopters and commandos, while British infantry dug in astride the road from Basra about twenty miles north of Kuwait.

Nothing happened, apart from a high casualty rate among the British forces as a result of the searing heat. The border between the two countries remained open, Kuwaiti and Iraqi businessmen operated as usual, and there were no new threats from Baghdad. As suddenly as they had arrived, the British began to pull out, to be replaced by an Arab peace force. Politicians stuck gamely to the story that the British deployment had averted an Iraqi invasion, while others held that the operation was partly a test of Britain's ability to move forces quickly – an unusually realistic hot weather manœuvre – and partly a means of reasserting national power in the wake of the Suez debacle five years earlier. It was certainly a show of strength in a region which had for so long been a British fiefdom.

On the Iraqi side it may all have been no more than an attempt to capitalize on the situation, and one which had few immediate consequences although Baghdad did persuade the Soviet Union to veto the newly-independent Kuwait's application for UN membership. In 1963, when the Qassem regime in Baghdad was overthrown by the Baathists, Iraq did formally recognize the independence of Kuwait – without accepting its boundaries – and also encouraged the Soviet Union to lift its veto on UN membership. The result was that, for the next twenty-seven years, Iraq sat with Kuwait in the UN and the Arab League, without ever questioning its sovereign status. Yet six days after the invasion of 2 August Iraq formally annexed Kuwait, declaring 'a comprehensive and eternal merger between the two countries'.

Over the years Iraq made several different claims to parts of Kuwait. In 1965, the Iraqis said they wanted the two islands of Warbah and Bubiyan 'along with other territory close to Iraq's border in such a way as to make the border line deeper inside Kuwait to create vital space necessary to construct the port at Umm Qasr and the railway line attached to it'. Iraq said it wanted agreement on these principles before it would agree to the formation of a border commission, for which the Kuwaitis were then pressing. The Kuwaitis refused, but did say that they would consider leasing the island of Warbah to Iraq for ninety-nine years.

In 1973 Iraq again tried to force the issue, this time by direct action as well as diplomatic belligerence. On 20 March two Iraqi armoured units occupied the Samita police station in Kuwait, without warning and without any indication as to what might come next. Acting with remarkable speed, the Kuwaitis mobilized not only their own small army, but also Arab and international opinion. Saudi Arabian forces moved into the emirate in a show of support, and Iran warned Iraq to pull out or face the consequences.

Faced with such concerted and determined opposition, the Iraqis quietly withdrew. More meetings followed, and in August 1973 Sheikh Jaber al-Ahmed, then the Kuwaiti prime minister, visited Baghdad for talks with Saddam Hussein, at this point still vice-president. This time the Iraqi side suggested the division of Bubiyan island into two, with the eastern part going to Iraq and the western staying as part of Kuwait. Again there was no agreement, but in subsequent talks the Iraqis appeared to accept Kuwait sovereignty over the areas they coveted.

In 1978 Izzat Ibrahim, Saddam's deputy, visited Kuwait and suggested that Iraq should rent half of Bubiyan. 'Iraq is committed to the principle that the border should be defined in such a way that it guarantees a naval position for Iraq, securing the defence necessary for its national interests and the Arab nation's interests in the Arabian Gulf,' he said.

In 1932, when Iraq gained its independence, Baghdad had appeared to accept the borders as defined by Sir Percy Cox at Uqair ten years earlier. Although like others before and after him, Nuri Said, the Iraqi prime minister, held that parts of Kuwait should come under Iraqi sovereignty, he formally accepted the boundaries in a letter to the British High Commissioner (number 2944 of 24 July). Iraqi apologists later said the letter had no legal standing because it was not ratified by the Iraqi legislature at that time. But Marc Weller, of the department of international law at Queens' College, Cambridge, has no doubt that the document is binding on Iraq. 'The fact it was not ratified is legally irrelevant,' he said.

If there is such a thing as the psychology of a state, then the psychology of Kuwait played a role in all that happened. Until 1961 it depended on Britain for its protection and over the next nine years still looked to its former protecting power. But from 1970 Kuwait was truly on its own, and evolved its own personal strategy for survival. Little bigger than Wales, with a population of less than two million – of which only 17 per cent were native-born Kuwaitis, and hence first class citizens – Kuwait had to live by its wits and its financial strength. So, alone among Gulf states, Kuwait established relations with both China and the Soviet Union, as well as America and the West. The most complete welfare state in the world was established, with free housing, sinecure jobs for the native-born, and free education (including overseas universities for the brightest), as well as such mundane items as free telephones, zero income taxes, and free medical services for all.

These measures helped ward off unrest from any deprived section of the community, but there was still a disaffected group, the 30 per cent of the population which was Shia. Most of these came from Iran, but some had origins in Iraq.

As in most Arab countries, the Shia were always regarded with suspicion and a certain amount of fear, but during the Gulf war they came to be seen as a potential Iranian fifth column. Because they were treated accordingly, they inevitably became resentful, and in some cases did carry out undercover operations on behalf of Iran. It was a dilemma for the authorities; if the Shia were left in the key positions which many had attained in the oil industry, then they might commit acts of sabotage. If they were removed, they became dissidents. In the event, the Kuwaiti government opted for a hard line, removing Shia from the armed forces and oil industry, deporting thousands, and silencing mosque leaders who spoke too openly in favour of the Islamic revolution in Iran.

There was reasonable cause for such measures. In 1985 a car laden with explosives was rammed into the emir's motorcade as he drove to his office. He escaped, but others were killed. Then bombs went off at the American and French embassies and other targets. Seventeen men of various nationalities were arrested, and all were found to belong to Daawa, the Iranian-backed group in Iraq opposed to Saddam Hussein. The men were sentenced to imprisonment, and in a few cases death, though no executions were carried out. The result was a steady succession of hijackings and kidnappings as Daawa and other groups sought to extricate their men. The plight of the Western hostages in Lebanon was directly linked to the fate of the Kuwait seventeen; Imad Mughniyah, one of the main hostage-takers in Beirut, was related to two of the men held in prison, and made the release of all seventeen a key bargaining tool for the return of the Westerners.

Having made sure that the wealth of the country was shared by all sections of the people, the Kuwaiti government hoped to buy off political resentment. The relative freedom of the press was one safety valve, again with reservations – a columnist on Al-Watan, the opposition newspaper, was ruefully amused when he found that the paper's resident censor was a civil servant half his age who had attended his lectures on political science at Kuwait University.

On a wider front, attempts at liberalization were always undermined by the very nature of the leadership of Kuwait's ruler, the al-Sabah. The al-Sabah are the leading representatives of the family system of government in the Arabian peninsula, pre-dating the Saudis and bearing comparison with the al-Thanis of Qatar or the Khalifahs of Bahrain. At present, the family consists of some 2,000 people, all of whom are linked in a complicated genealogy brought about by multiple marriages, the concubine system of the early years, and historic tribal links.

The first Sabah recorded as a ruler of Kuwait was in 1752, when the Utub, the tribe which occupied the area around the wells beside the sea, became independent of the Bani Khalid, the dominant group of the northern Arabian peninsula. Sheikh Jaber, the taciturn present ruler, is the direct descendant of that first sheikh. The al-Sabah, unlike the Saudis, do not style themselves kings and princes; the first ruler was chosen in a tribal majlis for his skill as an administrator and negotiator, and his successors have taken care not to assume any royal titles. 'Emir' can be translated as prince, but in Kuwait both the ruler and the ruled prefer the translation of leader, and (even if it is not always put into practice) suggest that the emir is merely a primus inter pares in the family.

Over the centuries in Kuwait, a partnership developed between the rulers and the leading merchant families. The power of the al-Sabah traditionally rested on their alliance with the al-Jaber, the leading merchant family of the early years, but today there is a wider network, with all the leading families of the country inter-locking in complicated relationships, and supporting each other for their mutual benefit. Of course there is corruption, in the sense that the leading families cream off commissions for themselves from foreign contracts, or divert state revenues to their own pockets. That is accepted so long as the welfare system is allowed to con-tinue. But there are still limits, which some of the younger members of the family sometimes exceeded, with consequent public grumbling when the assembly was sitting. There was a great deal of discontent when the young al-Sabahs insisted on taking over various ministries, apparently playing at politics for want of any-thing better to do. In the process they caused upsets and inefficien-cies in the administration, up to that point generally well run by expatriate Arabs, who were led by Palestinians.

Power at home has not, however, tempted Kuwait's leaders into decisions about their role in international politics. They accept that their country is a tiddler in international waters. The country's original name, Grane, is thought to be a diminutive of the Arab word qarn, a hill, and its modern name stems from the word kut, a small fort, which was built as a summer residence in Grane by Sheikh Barrak of the Bani Khalid about 1680.

Today nothing remains of the old town – everything was swept aside in the rush of building which took place in the 1970s and 1980s. Sheikh Jaber, the present ruler, presided over those boom years when he was crown prince and prime minister. Never a gregarious man – though he had a reputation as a minor playboy in his youth – he became ever more withdrawn as the cares of state pressed on him, and developed the habit of sitting silently at meetings, allowing those around him to do all the talking and then delivering a decision which brooked no argument.

In exile in Taif his manner disconcerted many a visiting American congressman. He would mumble a few words of greeting in Arabic and then leave the visitor to say his piece; the crown prince, Sheikh Saad, a more out-going man, was usually the one to keep things moving. In the swirl of white and gold, as the Kuwaiti ministers in exile maintained the semblance of a court and a government, American public relations men from Madison Avenue could be seen whispering in the ears of the exiles, and soon after would come some quotable quote, some new definition.

While we were in this unlovely Saudi Arabian hill town, Sheikh Saad was pressing the case for early action by Kuwait's allies: 'We do not care if our country is destroyed so long as it is liberated,' he said. 'We can build it again. What is left of Kuwait anyway after what Saddam's soldiers have done to it? As a citizen and an official, I am ready to sacrifice everything for the sake of regaining my land, of liberating Kuwait, and that is what every Kuwaiti thinks.' The emir looked silently on.

The assumption is often made that the emir speaks no English, an impression he is careful to foster, but diplomats have noted that when it suits him, he can converse quite well. Clearly, he picks his interlocutors: it was only when the Queen visited Kuwait that the resident British realized that the emir knew English. He held animated conversations with Her Majesty, but lapsed into Arabic when only embassy people were present.

Sheikh Jaber, who was born in 1926, was educated privately by a succession of Arab tutors, and first entered public service as governor of the oil port of Ahmadi when he was twenty-three. Then in

1963 he served as minister of finance and industry before becoming prime minister in 1965. He succeeded to the leadership in 1977, and three years later revived the National Assembly which had been suspended in 1976; he would close this down again because of the tensions caused by the Gulf war. In the early years of his rule Sheikh Jaber revived an idea of one of his ancestors. He would put on ordinary clothes and go alone to do a little shopping in the souk, both to check on prices and to gauge the mood of his state. On other occasions he would drive around the town in a Volkswagen car, although his official car was itself a relatively modest Chevrolet Caprice; that had to change after the attempt on his life by a suicide bomber in May 1985. Armour-plated Mercedes were then quickly imported, and it was in one of these that the emir fled his country in August.

The emir came to be regarded with respect but little affection. He was given credit for steering his country through the particularly difficult years of the Gulf war, and for setting up the Fund for Future Generations, the immensely successful scheme under which a proportion of each year's oil revenues were invested for the time when the oil runs out. The Fund is now estimated to be worth over $100 billion, and the interest on it financed Kuwait's government in exile.

Sheikh Jaber became more withdrawn as he grew older. He was virtually unknown to most of his subjects, and restricted himself to his own family – he has four wives – and to the other eighteen families who control 90 per cent of all Kuwaiti investments. There are stories about him, of course – most, in the Arab way, dealing with his sexual prowess: three of his wives are said to be relatively permanent, and the fourth consists of what one American female observer has described as 'the revolving slot'. He frequently marries some pretty bedouin girl, both for his own pleasure and as a way of cementing the alliance of the al-Sabah with the tribes. They need to be kept loyal to provide the security forces of the state, as poor in people as it is rich in oil. The tribes, in their turn, accept the largesse of the state but often continue their nomadic lifestyle. The emir did what he could to remedy the population problem: no one is quite sure of the exact total, but he is believed to have fathered thirty-six sons so far; the daughters have not been counted.

He became even more reclusive after the 1985 attempt on his life, travelled rarely and, when he did, took bottled water with him and always employed a food taster; the style accorded with his natural instincts. Unlike other Arab potentates – and many of his own family – Sheikh Jaber shunned ostentation. He wore a cheap watch rather than the Rolex usually favoured, and he had a reputation for being careful, to say the least; many of his subjects claimed he was downright mean, more concerned with his personal fortune – estimated at $2 billion – than with the good of the state. His record on the Fund for Future Generations belies that, but he certainly became one of the richest men in the world, with investments in many countries – all overseen by one of his displaced subjects, a Palestinian financier.

For all his moderation, the emir had some strong dislikes, and one of the chief among them was his host in exile, King Fahd. This stemmed from one of the early Gulf Co-operation Council conferences. The emir is a morning man, rising early to say his prayers and often getting to his office soon after 6 a.m.; by midday work is done, leaving the afternoon and evening for relaxation. At the GCC meeting in Muscat, the final plenary session was scheduled for 10 a.m.; officials and distinguished guests were in their places, and at the appointed time, the heads of state made their dignified entrance. All except King Fahd; after fifteen minutes of increasing annoyance, an emissary was dispatched to the king's suite. He returned to announce that his majesty was sleeping. The heads of state marched crossly out, and hung about for a couple of hours until the king finally woke up – no one dared to call him. Eventually, the conference was held, but the annoyance of the emir lasted well after he had returned to his own country.

In its external relations, Kuwait showed the most sophistication of any of the Gulf states. As a Kuwaiti minister told us long before the events of 1990: 'Our policy is governed by the knowledge that our country is surrounded by three of the nastiest regimes in the world.' There was no love lost among any of them; Saudi Arabia viewed with apprehension and dismay Kuwait's experiments with democracy, fearing that their neighbour's example would have to be followed, a prospect which filled the ruling family with dread. In Iraq there were not only the historic territorial claims trotted out at all opportune moments, there was also a real desire for protected access to the Gulf through possession of the islands of Warbah and Bubiyan, and resentment at Kuwait tapping into the rich Rumaileh oilfield. And Iran saw Kuwait as the natural target for Ayatollah Khomeini's Islamic revolution – a rich, effete country with a substantial group of Shia ready to take over and establish reforms along lines laid down in Tehran.

Alarmed by the Iranian threat as early as 1979, Kuwait gave its quiet backing to Saddam Hussein as he orchestrated the border incidents with Iran; and once the invasion of Iran was launched on 22 September 1980, it gave its full support to Baghdad. Iraqi planes were allowed to overfly Kuwaiti territory, and Kuwait became virtually an Iraqi port, replacing Basra as the entry point for war material.

Like the other Gulf states, the Kuwaitis believed that the Iraqi armies would be able to subdue the disorganized Iranian troops with ease. And again, earlier than most, they also realized that this was not to be. By 1982 they had begun to make their dispositions for the future and attempted to distance themselves from the more excessive rhetoric coming out of Baghdad. Kuwait became an enthusiastic member of the Gulf Co-operation Council, a regional grouping which pointedly excluded Iraq, and also improved its relations with Oman, a former opponent which was now seen as useful in the light of its good relations with Iran.

In the war against Iran, Iraq had shown itself to be a protector of doubtful competence; what was more, Baghdad had drawn Iran into a 'tanker war' in which Kuwaiti shipping was a prime casualty. Although one of the raisons d'être of the Gulf Co-operation Council had been to keep the superpowers out of the Gulf, the Kuwaitis sought security for the future by encouraging US intervention, suggesting that their ships be put under the US flag as a protection against the marauding Iranians. The Americans hesitated, so without fanfare the Kuwaitis approached the Soviets, who immediately agreed to charter them Russian ships, a proposal which would necessitate the presence of protective Soviet naval forces. In these closing days of the Cold War, the Soviet Union was only too happy to have a valid excuse to increase its presence in the Gulf.

But the Kuwaiti approach to Moscow had merely been calculated to provoke a US response. Once Washington recognized the possibility of the Soviet navy dominating the Gulf, it took the Kuwaiti bait, put aside its earlier reservations and agreed to the Kuwaiti request for naval protection. On 21 July 1987, the first Kuwaiti tanker hoisted the stars and stripes and sailed into the Gulf with an American captain. It proved a largely symbolic gesture since the USS *Bridgeton* hit a mine on its inward voyage, and the more fragile escorting American warships had to huddle behind the massive tanker for protection as they headed up to Kuwait.

The Kuwaiti intention was two-fold: they sought immediate protection for their vessels, but in the long term they wanted an American guarantee for their country. The Kuwaitis feared an Iranian victory in the Gulf and therefore financed Saddam. But they also recognized more clearly than most, that a victorious Saddam would be a danger. Sheikh Ali Khalifa, then the oil minister, told us at the time that Kuwait hoped America would remain in the Gulf once hostilities were over. It was a wish shared by the Saudis, anxious about Iranian intentions and nervous about the Shia minorities in the eastern provinces of the kingdom where the oil-fields were situated.

At the end of the war in 1988, Kuwait and Saudi Arabia had different perceptions of the dangers the region would face: the Saudis argued that the main threat still came from Iran, while Kuwait felt that Iran was so debilitated by eight years of war that it presented no real threat, and that Iraq, still mobilized and aggressive, might well give trouble. So Kuwait moved quickly to repair its relations with Tehran, and found its assessment justified. The Iranians immediately agreed to restore diplomatic ties, and to put aside the quarrels which only a year earlier had led to rocket attacks on Kuwaiti installations from Iranian positions in the occupied Fao peninsula.

The Saudis expressed dissatisfaction at the Kuwait–Iran rapprochement, and during the 1989 pilgrimage put pressure on the emirate by arresting a number of Kuwaiti pilgrims, accusing them of setting off bombs in Mecca. Saudi Arabia did not take kindly to Kuwait's policy, which placated Iran while relying on America to defend it against Iraq – Kuwait having invested much of its oil wealth in America, for political as well as commercial reasons.

As Iraqi pressure on Kuwait mounted in spring 1990, the emirate seized on what it saw as an opportunity to settle once and for all the outstanding issues with Iraq: in return for a debt write-off and compensation payments, there should be a final demarcation of the border between the two countries and a promise of non- aggression by Iraq, perhaps even a mutual pact. Kuwait was emboldened to take this high-risk approach because Iraq had already offered the emirate a non-aggression treaty in return for border adjustments, which would have included ceding Warbah and Bubiyan islands as well as the frontier strip which would have given Iraq the whole of the oilfield. Now Kuwait thought that, in view of its agreement in principle to a treaty in exchange for territorial demarcation and money, Iraq would enter into negotiations which might end in a compromise.

When the Iraqi tanks finally rolled in on 2 August it was as much of a shock to the Gulf and the Arab world as it was to the West. Newspapers throughout the region had been full of the Iraq–Kuwait issue for weeks, yet leaders and diplomats still clung to the belief that one Arab country would never seize by force the territory of another. The row between the two countries was 'a passing cloud', the papers said; it was a family quarrel, something which could be settled among the Arabs with no need for outside interference.

This was not an unreasonable attitude: disputes among the Arab states had been innumerable since Britain abandoned its east of Suez role in 1971, yet they had never spilled over into warfare. Always the confrontation had been with non-Arab countries – with

Iran, or with Israel and America, or with China when it backed Omani rebels in Dhofar. Surely no Arab state would deliberately and without provocation invade and seize another?

When that happened, the statelets of the Gulf reacted in the same way as their senior partner, Saudi Arabia. They wanted protection, and they wanted it fast. The United Arab Emirates, in particular, suddenly realized that they ranked second only to Kuwait on the Iraqi list of those who had damaged Baghdad. When American and British envoys arrived to ask for the support of these small states for the embargo they were putting in place, they were met with promises that everything possible would be done, and with permission for the West to arrange a physical presence in their territory.

Qatar, the state most ideologically and temperamentally akin to Saudi Arabia, requested and was given American air force units for its defence. The United Arab Emirates told Britain that RAF planes could use their airports, and British instructors and equipment would train their small forces to deal with possible chemical attack.

Oddly enough, it was Oman, the country generally regarded as still something of a British protectorate, which took the most independent line. Oman had British seconded and contract officers in all its military services, and it had allowed America to position stores on Masirah island and at Thamrait on the edge of the Empty Quarter. It also welcomed British and American aircraft, including the B52 bombers which US air force chiefs boasted could 'carpet-bomb Iraq'. Yet Oman still took a softer line than most other Gulf states. Just as it had maintained links with Iran throughout the Gulf war while also drawing closer to Egypt, Iraq's close ally, so now Oman tried to steer between the most extreme positions of its allies and neighbours, quietly backing its neighbour Yemen in that country's attempts to find a compromise between the parties.

Yemen itself was in a difficult position. Only a few months earlier the long-divided northern and southern sectors of the country had been united, with ministers from the Marxist south now serving in the government beside the more pragmatic and nationalist men from the north. The southerners, with their seafaring tradition and alliance with Moscow, itself until then the patron of Iraq, were more inclined to side with Baghdad in the dispute. The northerners, closer to Saudi Arabia and more aware of the damage that kingdom could inflict, took a more cautious line. The result was that the government in Sanaa allowed Iraqi planes to continue to fly into the Yemen, sent some food and other goods to Baghdad, and resisted pressure to align itself with Saudi Arabia.

This caused tremendous damage to the country's fragile economy. Saudi Arabia withdrew many of the privileges the 1.5 million Yemenis living in the kingdom had enjoyed, forcing thousands of them to go home, reducing the remittances sent to Yemen and putting a severe strain on services there. At the same time the Saudis again distributed money and arms to the tribes on the Saudi side of the border with Yemen, encouraging them to resume their traditional sport of harassing Yemeni government troops and installations, and seizing what booty they could find.

Saudi Arabia always aspired to be the dominant power in the lower Gulf, while Iran and Iraq vied for influence in the north. Between them, these three countries could theoretically produce nearly 20 million barrels of oil a day at full capacity. Together with Kuwait, it is estimated that by the end of the century they will account for more than thirty per cent of world oil production, with the largest increases in output coming from Iraq and Kuwait.

Better conservation measures and the development of alternative energy sources may help to slow the world's appetite for oil but, as other sources dry up, Gulf supplies will inevitably come to dominate the market. At the time of the Kuwait invasion, western Europe was taking 35 per cent of its oil from the Gulf and Japan 77 per cent. America had cut its imports, although it still took 5 per cent of its crude requirements from the region. But it is not the present which the oil consumers worry about – rather the uncertain future: the Gulf oil reservoir is not only the largest in the world, its proven reserves are actually increasing with new exploration. Known supplies will last well into the second half of the next century, while Qatar alone has liquid gas reserves which would last for the next 300 years at present rates of extraction.

In Saudi Arabia, it was the Americans who found the first

deposits and brought in the wells, and they who set up the refineries and distribution system. The Americans also financed the kingdom's first faltering years as a sovereign state. The result has been a symbiotic relationship between Washington and Riyadh, although direct American control over oil production and distribution has been replaced by diplomatic leverage. Saudi Arabia became America's one dependable ally in the Arab world, a country which always took the moderate course, and which in the final phase of the Cold War remained firmly in the Western camp. Not until two months after the Iraqi invasion of Kuwait did the Saudis agree to restore diplomatic relations with the Soviet Union, something Moscow had been seeking for years.

One of the main fears of the Saudi government was its own Shia minority in the eastern province. That area of the country was always policed with greater force than any other region and Sunni administrators and middle managers from other parts of the country were installed, rather than local people. There were frequent disturbances, usually put down with bloodshed and loss of life and never publicized in the kingdom or in the West.

The Americans were isolated from all this. The Aramco people lived in their own compounds around Dahran – American suburbs set down in the Saudi Arabian desert, complete with entertainment US-style. They had their own television station, American cafés and restaurants, American schools, and all-American values. Only alcohol was absent, in deference to the strict Saudi ban on drink, but Aramco did employ a welfare officer who offered advice on how to make homemade wines and beers, and how to avoid making oneself blind with some of the less-successful concoctions. There was also a tacit arrangement under which any American found drunk in public, or sharing a bottle with a local employee, was quietly shipped out to Bahrain just thirty minutes flying time away – a company jet was always on stand-by. The penalty was dismissal, but this was a lot better than the prison terms or floggings which many British and other nationals received when they were caught.

Throughout the Gulf war the Saudis poured money into

Baghdad, probably more than $20 billion by the end of the war. Unlike the Kuwaitis, the Saudis did not even suggest that Iraq should repay this amount; they knew that the Iraqis would not be able to do so, and instead sought to use the cash to ensure Baghdad's friendship in the future. This was a central plank of Saudi diplomacy: aware of their own weakness, the Saudis always relied on wealth to secure their aims.

As a result of their conservative religious outlook, rigidly enforced by the powerful fundamentalist Wahabi sect, the Saudis had always tried to keep the Americans at arm's length. The jargon phrase was 'an over-the-horizon presence' – the American navy comfortingly close if it was needed, but far enough away not to have any impact on the slow pace of Saudi social life. Worried about Iranian intentions, both under the Shah and during the Islamic revolution, the Saudis spent billions in building up their own armed forces, buying the most advanced aircraft from Britain, tanks from America, ships from Italy and armoured vehicles from France. The kingdom was the greatest arms market in the world, fully able to pay cash for its purchases even after the slump in oil prices, and willing to buy almost anything on offer. Yet no amount of money could purchase security, for Saudi Arabia lacked one essential requirement – manpower.

The Saudi population today is probably about 11 million, with up to 2 million Yemenis and a million other immigrants in the kingdom. That is only a few million short of the Iraqi total, yet while the Iraqis have managed for a decade to put a million-strong army in the field, the Saudis cannot manage half that total. The difference is in the structure of their societies; Iraq was until recently a poor country, where the army offered the prospect of a secure and reasonable living to a young man, and the prospect of political and professional advancement to the more ambitious. In Saudi Arabia, everyone had been rich for the past two generations; the well-off and well-educated saw little future in serving in an army they did not believe would ever have to fight, and which they knew could never lead to political advantage. Flying fast planes in the air force may have been an attraction to some, but the army rarely was, and they certainly considered the technical branches of the services beneath them. The result was that Pakistanis had to be brought in to run the technical branches – and at one time a whole Pakistani division was stationed on the South Yemen border to guard against trouble from that Marxist country. In 1990, the Pakistani division sent to help in the defence of Saudi Arabia was once again posted on the Yemeni border.

The bedouin, who did feel that carrying a gun and wearing a uniform was a reasonable occupation, gravitated to the National Guard, originally set up as an accessory to the regular forces, but lately an integral though more lightly armed part of the kingdom's defence structure. So there was never any real hope that the Saudis could defend themselves. Just like the Kuwaitis, the idea was that the army would act as a trip-wire in case of invasion, and give time for international opinion and practical help to be mobilized. A further factor was that Iraq was never seen as a potential enemy. First on the list was Iran, which meant that coastal defences had to be built up; secondly came the threat of a land attack from Yemen, and thirdly that of air attack by Israel. Separated from Iraq by the sovereign state of Kuwait, the Saudi planners, such as they were, did not even consider aggression by Baghdad.

So when Dick Cheney, the American secretary of defence, flew into Riyadh on 6 August to offer American help in deterring an attack from the Iraqi forces in Kuwait, the Saudis had little idea of what to do. They were totally dependent on America for their intelligence, apart from what their own forward troops on the ground were telling them. The Americans showed them satellite pictures which, they said, demonstrated that Iraqi tanks and armoured columns were preparing to invade the kingdom. King Fahd, Prince Sultan, the defence minister, and Prince Abdullah, the crown prince, solemnly examined the aerial pictures handed round by the Americans and passed them to their aides. Most likely none of them could tell a tank column on a satellite picture from a string of camels in the desert; nonetheless, all looked suitably solemn and impressed. And as expected, they asked for the help the Americans were determined to give.

A second invasion was approved, an invasion of the Arabian peninsula by the Americans and their allies.

The Arabs

For many of the young Americans thrown so unexpectedly into a conflict no one had foreseen, their new surroundings were as strange as anything imagined in Hollywood.

In the first few weeks, it was like something out of *Lawrence of Arabia* as they found themselves confined to tented camps in the desert or quartered in barracks in Masirah or other holding areas – although many of the tents and the barrack rooms were air-conditioned. Then, when they were allowed to go into nearby towns, Khafji, perhaps, or Jubail, they found some things they were used to, supermarkets, milkbars, but a peculiar absence of others – bars, cinemas, and chemists. Most noticeable of all was that the only women to be seen were dressed in enveloping black, moving purposefully with children in tow or walking deferentially behind their men.

This was a new world for the GIs, but one for which the Americans had tried to brief them, warning them to be polite, not to whistle at women, or to try to meet on equal terms with the men, or act with the usual American openness as they took their first glimpses of this new civilization. Even more difficult for many young Americans was the new perception of Arabs as a friendly people; until the invasion of Kuwait, many Americans had been brought up to think of Israel as the one dependable ally in the Middle East, to assume that all Arabs were enemies who wanted to eliminate Israel once and for all. Overnight, that idea had to change. There were no longer simply Arabs, but good Arabs and bad Arabs, and even some in-between Arabs.

The adjustment was even more difficult for the Saudis. Suddenly they saw women soldiers driving trucks, or even taking off their jackets to mend punctures at the side of the road. They heard of rabbis accompanying the troops, of kosher food being flown in, and then too of bacon for breakfast. The culture shock was mutual. Saudi Arabia, with its adherence to the strict doctrine of Wahabism, was in many ways a hypocritical country: the 5,000 members of the ruling family and the senior officers of state conformed in public, but did as they wished behind the high walls of their villas. The prohibition on drink did not apply to them, and while their women dressed in enveloping black when they went out, they wore designer jeans or high fashion dresses at home, and the videos they watched would not have been shown in public even if cinemas had been allowed in the kingdom.

King Fahd himself, in his youth a playboy who drank, gambled and womanized, had matured into an experienced statesman and administrator, yet he still found it difficult to concentrate for long periods on affairs of state, and would take off in his desert caravan for sudden holidays, leaving the papers mounting on his desk, decisions still to be taken and appointments unmade.

He took the title of Custodian of the Two Holy Places rather than that of king to emphasize his guardianship of Mecca and Medina, and to win respect among the growing number of Islamic fundamentalists in his own country and in Iran. The king was in theory an absolute monarch, and he had quietly dropped the promise made a few years earlier of establishing a majlis al-shura, an advisory council, though the idea was suddenly revived in November 1990, no doubt in deference to American democratic tastes. But as head of a large ruling group, the king could not rule by decree. Though Fahd and the chief ministers were more equal than other princes, they still had to take note of the opinions of the rest of the family, and to make sure that decisions were acceptable to the great mass of the people.

In August 1990, there were divisions within this ruling group: Prince Abdullah, the crown prince, who was always close to Syria and antagonistic towards Iraq, favoured immediate action; Prince Sultan, the defence minister, was more wary of American intentions, either in spite of or because of the fact that his son, Prince Bandar, was the Saudi ambassador in Washington. And King Fahd himself was almost obsessed with the price of oil, desperate to see that the country's income was enough to carry through all the development projects he had initiated, and which he saw as the means to maintain stability.

The king viewed the Iraqi invasion not so much as a moral outrage, or an offence against international law, but rather as a major commercial threat, an act which rocked the whole structure of international commerce, and which, if not rectified, would make it impossible for the kingdom to continue on its prosperous course. Significantly, the only time King Fahd was seen to show genuine emotion was when he made a television speech in which he had to announce a budget deficit and reveal that the kingdom would have to borrow money on the international market; that did bring tears to his eyes.

King Fahd felt personally responsible for oil politics and oil affairs. There was an oil minister, Hisham Nazer, but unlike his predecessor, Sheikh Zaki Yamani, he was there merely to carry out the king's instructions. The king's style was to achieve consensus. He would wait and nudge until his views prevailed, only rarely showing outright displeasure with ministers. If one proved inefficient, he would move the task to another; sackings were rare. Of those which did take place, the most dramatic came in 1986 when the king dismissed Yamani, best known of all Arab oil ministers, and the architect of the Gulf Arab producers' policy. Yamani took the international rather than the nationalist view, and sought a balance between fair returns for producers, and fair prices for the consumers who supplied most of the manufactured goods the oil states needed. However, Yamani's approach was not bringing Saudi Arabia the income the king wanted, and so Yamani had to go. Once the king himself was dictating policy to his oil minister, Saudi Arabia embarked on a course which quickly raised the price. But Yamani's predictions came true, and at one point oil sank as low as $8 a barrel.

In 1990 Iraq was determined to push the oil price up in order to fund its post-war reconstruction programme and keep a restive population content. Two countries in particular, Kuwait and the United Arab Emirates, were depressing the oil price by massive over-production – pumping much more oil than the quotas allotted to them by OPEC. The Kuwait policy, laid down by Sheikh Ali Khalifa, the oil minister, was well considered and logical: Kuwait had invested its huge wealth in down-stream oil activities: refineries, filling stations, and petro-chemical industries. It saw maximum profit in maximum production, earning higher revenues for itself by expanding its market share rather than by raising prices; there was no point in Kuwait having to pay dearly for crude for its ancillary interests. So at times Kuwait was producing one million barrels a day more than its quota, and the emirates too were going as high as this – in this case it was because the two main producers, Abu Dhabi and Dubai, each wanted to maximize cash flow in order to outdo one another in development projects.

To Iraq, such behaviour by Kuwait and the emirates was corroboration of its xenophobic suspicions. To restore order to the oil market, the Iraqis suggested early in 1990 that a conference should be held at which the excesses of Kuwait and the emirates would be discussed. Saudi Arabia, the traditional fence-sitter, would attend, along with Iraq. But while agreeing to attend, Saudi Arabia worked hard behind the scenes to arrange a common front of Gulf oil producers against Iraq, fearful as usual that efforts to push up prices would anger the Americans. And in a remarkable transcript of a telephone conversation between King Fahd and Sheikh Khalifah al-Thani, the emir of Qatar, made on 9 July 1990, the plot was revealed. It was a triumph for the Iraqi intelligence service, which obtained the intercept, and it did seem to show, as the Iraqis claimed, that an anti-Iraqi front was being formed, apparently to arrange matters in advance of the OPEC meeting scheduled for later that month. It also gave a believable picture of Saudi worries and fears.

King Fahd began the conversation: 'We have had enough. Israel threatens Iraq and now Iraq threatens Israel. Now we're back to the same old story of Nasser before 1967. We want to think the matter over. God bless you.'

Sheikh Khalifah replied: 'God protect you. I shall always be with you.'

FAHD: God bless you. I wanted to tell you that I told Hisham [Nazer, Saudi oil minister] to tell his brothers the ministers not to pay attention to what the Iraqi minister said. Iraq is in trouble. There's a sensitive situation between Iraq and Israel. Every day we are worried by something. The Iraqi minister said some meaningless words. The important thing is we put everything in order during these two months, especially when things become quiet, and we follow a defensive stand. Two months are left to us. As Gulf states, we shall meet and organize matters. The same applies to Iraq. The Iraqis have lost their temper. Now they are talking in on way or another. They have lost their temper. And you know that when someone loses his temper his speech is unreasonable.

KHALIFAH: True, their speech is unreasonable.

FAHD: We don't want that.

KHALIFAH: I am sure it is unreasonable.

FAHD: We don't want problems with Israel. We don't want problems with Iran.

KHALIFAH: True.

FAHD: But we are envied as Gulf states. Yet where were those who now envy us when we were poor? They did not say our brothers have nothing.

KHALIFAH: No, they did not.

FAHD: And when we became rich we did not stop helping them.

KHALIFAH: They know us only when we have something. Otherwise, they did not know us.

FAHD: When we were poor, riding donkeys and finding difficulties in coming across a date no one asked about us. And since we became rich we have not stopped helping them.

KHALIFAH: God bless you.

FAHD: All I want to do is stop the bad temper. When things become quiet it will be easy to talk to Iraq. Saddam thinks highly of you. All we must do is to stop this bad temper. I told my minister to meet their minister in Iraq tomorrow. Before you meet with Iraq, all of you must agree as Gulf ministers. Keep quiet even if the Iraqi minister says something bad. These people, the Iraqis, have got themselves into a problem with Israel, but they have nothing to do with Israel. Seven hundred kilometres separate them from Israel. The matters must be dealt with wisely.

KHALIFAH: What you say is quite true.

FAHD: And our brothers in Iraq have put themselves into a maze.

KHALIFAH: That's true.

FAHD: They have given themselves the same problems as Nasser, and he could not solve them. How can we fight the whole world? Between us, I think the Palestinians have pushed matters too far. They are losing nothing.

KHALIFAH: True.

FAHD: I hope Abu Ammar [Yasser Arafat] will be reasonable. I told our brothers the Palestinians that we will do our best so that we might not lose the West Bank and Gaza. I don't want to see the West Bank and Gaza lost by sheer words.

KHALIFAH: That's disastrous.

FAHD: You must be reasonable and think carefully. Look at the Soviet Union. Who ever thought the Soviet Union would reach such an agreement with the US?

King Fahd suggested the Iraqis were calling the conference while the Ruler of Qatar would be away. 'As a principle, if they had that idea, I said it can't be. Let oil ministers first meet and discuss with each other. It will be better if ministers of oil, foreign affairs and finance meet in every country to discuss the matters from all political, financial, social and petroleum aspects.'

KHALIFAH: True.

FAHD: At that time you might think of a summit meeting. But don't think of holding a summit if there's a chance of failure.

KHALIFAH: And Kuwait?

FAHD: Probably our brothers the Iraqis will agree to dismiss the idea of a summit meeting.

KHALIFAH: Thank God.

FAHD: It's easy to start a conflict but it is very difficult to stop it. Israel is our number one nightmare. It has 200 nuclear warheads and forty-seven atom bombs. Its people are crazy. All our Palestinian brothers have to do is to do their best and we will help them. They have got to put their hand on the West Bank and Gaza. They don't have to go to the extreme. In that case Israel would make them real colonies.

KHALIFAH: We have to gain one position after another.

Several things emerge from all this. The first is the way Saudi Arabia is acknowledged as the leader of the Gulf oil states, able to impose its will and its policies on others; second is that – as Iraq believed – there really was a conspiracy to avoid a summit meeting at which, in effect, Kuwait and the emirates would be in the dock for their over-production. Third, perhaps, is an insight into the self-pitying attitude of the rich oil countries, who rightly believed they were loved only for their money, yet apparently sought to be wanted for themselves. A strange idea of realpolitik, though not so strange as the image of King Fahd wandering the desert on a donkey searching for a date-palm.

There were other divisions in the Gulf. Soon after the end of the Gulf war, President Saddam had taken the initiative in setting up the Arab Co-operation Council grouping Iraq, Jordan, Egypt and Yemen. Saudi Arabia was not included. The idea was to harness Egypt's millions of workers, Jordan's expertise and its ability to talk to the West, and Iraq's oil and potential wealth. Yemen was included, the Saudis feared, merely to apply pressure on them in the southern part of the peninsula. The ACC did make some economic sense, but it was also a counterweight to the Gulf Co-operation Council made up of all the 'traditional' countries of the Gulf, and dominated by Saudi Arabia. Even within that group of six states, there were differences: Saudi Arabia saw Iran still as the potential aggressor, Oman and the emirates were anxious to establish friendly relations with that country, and Kuwait as usual wanted to buy off all possible threats. Qatar, as the emir's dutiful conversation with King Fahd showed, was anxious only to do what Saudi Arabia wanted.

One of the great difficulties was that no one knew just where Iran was going. President Rafsanjani of Iran was committed to opening his country to the West, realizing that the Soviet Union was preoccupied with its own troubles and in no shape to help. He understood that to repair the damage of eight years of war and restore his country's shattered economy, Western investment and Western know-how were desperately needed. But within Iran other powerful voices argued against this: Ahmad Khomeini, the old man's son, and Ali Akbar Mohtashemi, the former interior minister, led a faction which opposed any opening to the West and advocated a dogmatic adherence to the line laid down by the founder of the revolution. They cared not at all, they claimed, for the physical well-being of the people; what mattered was their spiritual life. Even if this was no more than a rationalization of their struggle for power, the outcome was always in doubt, which meant that other countries had to take a wary view of possible Iranian reactions. The picture was further complicated by the wavering policy of the new spiritual leader of the nation, Ayatollah Ali Khamenei.

Away from the Gulf, in the northern tier of states, the Arab–Israel issue remained the central problem, but with the end of the Gulf war and the advent of the Bush administration in 1988 this had entered a new phase. Bush and James Baker, the secretary of state, sought a settlement of this last major regional problem, and they recognized that, if this were to be achieved, the Palestinians had to derive advantage from it. The stubborn efforts of the Israeli prime minister, Yitzhak Shamir, to postpone action could not go on for ever.

But as Washington pursued its policy of dialogue with the PLO, the Palestinians were drifting towards Iraq. Though the PLO was still ostensibly based in Tunis, its headquarters were in fact in Baghdad, and the organization was becoming more and more dependent on Saddam for political backing as well as material support. Just as it seemed the diplomatic process might be getting somewhere, Abu Abbas, the pro-Iraqi leader of the PLO-affiliated Arab Liberation Front, made a seaborne raid on a crowded Israeli beach, an event which caused the Americans to call off the Tunis talks. Naturally enough the expansionist Iraqi regime saw the PLO as one more ally – it is a full member of the Arab League – but also as a puppet group to be manipulated, often in order to embarrass Syria, the rival Baath stronghold in the area.

As for Syria, Iraq's dispute with the rival Baath party in Damascus had never been resolved. The Iraqis took their dispute with Syria seriously: not only was Damascus a political rival, it had also sided with Iran during the eight years of war, and had to be punished. So as well as doing what it could to push the PLO into action against Syria in south Lebanon, the Iraqis also shipped arms, including tanks, to General Michel Aoun, the Maronite leader in the small Christian enclave north of Beirut, from where he shelled Syrian positions in the western half of the city.

On 13 October, the Syrians were finally able to deal with this irritation. After an artillery pounding of his palace and his positions in east Beirut, General Aoun took refuge in the French embassy. He had always said he would die with honour rather than surrender; in the event, he gave in rather easily. It was clear that the United States had given Syria the go-ahead to impose its control in Christian Lebanon while France, the traditional supporter of the Christians, did nothing except to take in the general and his family. Equally, the Israelis took no part. It was a warning to Saddam.

In all the constant politicking of the Arab world at this time, Saddam Hussein alone had a clear idea of what he was trying to do: he saw himself as the new Nasser, the leader of the Arab world from the Mediterranean to the Indian Ocean, from the Atlantic to the Gulf. He realized that the only way to attain that position, in the long run, would be to take on Israel, the one uniting factor in Arab politics, but he also knew that this required even greater military capability.

Saddam's great rival, President Hafez al-Assad of Syria, had always sought to give his country 'strategic parity' with Israel; but he had been abandoned by his Soviet patrons in 1988, and given Syria's chronically depressed economy, had no chance of getting the arms he needed. Saddam Hussein already had them; for most of the Gulf war, the Soviet Union kept up its supplies to Iraq, and France, Germany, Italy, Britain and a dozen countries of the Far East and Latin America made sure he had all he needed to stop the export of the Islamic revolution. Once the war was over, it was easier still, as companies around the world competed for Iraqi arms orders, and Saddam continued his quest for nuclear capability. Above all, Saddam had chemical weapons, and had shown, during the Gulf war and immediately afterwards in Kurdistan, that he was prepared to use them. Dubbed the poor man's atom bomb, chemical weapons were easy to make, relatively easy to use, and devastating in their effect – the psychological impact alone was worth a couple of divisions.

In the last years of the Gulf war, the Iraqis had also concentrated on developing their missile technology, lobbing rockets into Tehran and other Iranian cities, just as the Iranians hit Baghdad, Basra and other towns. Now reports coming out of Baghdad spoke of new, long-range rockets, and warheads adapted to take poison gas. It mattered not at all that the rockets were inaccurate, in fact, that was something of an advantage: it would be possible to claim to have been aiming at troop concentrations if a rocket and gas attack happened to lay waste the centre of Tel Aviv. The Israelis took the threat seriously, holding gas drills and early in October 1990 beginning to issue gas masks to the whole of the population – except the Palestinians of the West Bank and Gaza, who were required to pay.

The Israelis were undoubtedly worried, and earlier in the year had openly discussed destroying Iraq's chemical capability. It was this talk of attacking Iraqi targets which prompted Saddam Hussein's speech in which he threatened 'to cause fire to devour half of Israel if Iraq were attacked'. That conditional clause was usually omitted by the Israelis, and by the Americans, who issued stiff warnings to the Iraqi leader. In fact, at that time, Saddam Hussein was far more frightened by Israel than Israel was by Baghdad. Like the Saudis, he knew the Israelis had nuclear warheads and bombs, and understood that they would not hesitate to use them; what Saddam was trying to do was to use the threat of Israel to unite the Arabs under his leadership. In the long run, he no doubt saw himself as the liberator of Jerusalem, the Arab leader who gave the Palestinians a homeland; but his dream was not of conquest, but of becoming so strong that the Israelis would think it necessary to negotiate.

There was another thread to Saddam's strategy. The Baath party had always put the emphasis on pan-Arabism – the two most senior bodies in Iraq were the national command of the Baath party, dealing with pan-Arab affairs, and the regional command, dealing only with Iraq. With the end of the war came a new stress on the ideal of pan-Arabism, of shared responsibility to confront Israel or any other threats to the Arabs. But there was a corollary: not only should the burdens be spread over the whole Arab nation, but also the benefits. In other words, the rich oil states should share their wealth with their poorer brethren. Saddam Hussein put the argument forward merely to try to get more help out of Saudi Arabia, Kuwait or the smaller Gulf states; he did not appear to have considered that with the second greatest oil reserves in the Middle East, his own country might one day have to start financing the poorer Arab countries.

Certainly Iraq did subsidize the PLO, handing over as much as $200 million in the years after Yasser Arafat effectively moved his headquarters from Tunis to Baghdad; but that was for a particular political purpose, and any idea of general altruism was a long way from Saddam's mind.

By far the most complicated problem Saddam faced was his relations with Iran. In 1988 Ayatollah Khomeini had been forced by the economic circumstances of his country, and his army's inability to go on fighting, to 'drink the poisoned chalice' – to accept UN Resolution 598 establishing a ceasefire and setting out a loose timetable for troop withdrawals, exchange of prisoners and normalization of relations. But two years after the formal end of the war, the Iraqis still had no peace treaty with Iran, their troops were at battle stations along the 720-mile border, and prisoners of war on both sides remained in their camps.

When hostilities began in 1980, Saddam Hussein made the resolution of the border dispute a prime war aim, and yet in 1990 he gave away all that the Iraqi soldiers thought they had been fighting for. On 15 August Saddam sent a letter to Rafsanjani giving the Iranians everything they wanted: the border to be down the middle of the Shatt al-Arab, withdrawal from all occupied Iranian territory, and an immediate exchange of prisoners. In his letter Saddam Hussein did not try to disguise what had been done:

Dear Brother President Rafsanjani. Everything has become clear and everything you wanted and concentrated upon has been realized. All that is left is to publicize the documents so that we together can look from an honourable position towards a new life in which co-operation prevails under the shadow of Islamic principles, and that each of us respects the rights of the other and keeps away those fishing in muddy waters on our shores. Perhaps we could co-operate in preserving the Gulf as a lake of peace and stability free from foreign fleets and powers which are lurking, in addition to other fields of life.

The Iraqi letter not only gave Iran all it wanted, but it played on Tehran's suspicions of the American presence in the Gulf. Iran was swift to condemn the Iraqi invasion of Kuwait, and said it would impose all the sanctions called for by the UN, but it was also deeply critical of the huge build-up of American forces, and feared that such a massive presence would not end with the withdrawal of Iraq from Kuwait. Iran, like other Gulf states, always sought to exclude the superpowers from the area, and if it could not continue the Shah's role as the policeman of the Gulf, it was willing to share control with Iraq and Saudi Arabia, so long as no one state became dominant, and all agreed to keep out external powers. That was the prospect which Saddam Hussein cleverly held out in his letter.

Saddam's intention, of course, was to remove the threat on his eastern border, and enable his army to concentrate on the south. Some 24 Iraqi divisions, 300,000 soldiers, were deployed along the border with Iran; two days after Saddam sent his letter to Tehran, those troops began to move to Kuwait and the south of the country, with a few divisions in the north wheeling round to increase the guard on the Turkish and Syrian borders. The Iran–Iraq frontier was left to police and border guards, with the crossing points suddenly open. Not only had Saddam Hussein arranged the removal of a military threat, he had also gone a long way towards ensuring that the UN embargo could never be really effective.

Saddam had done much the same thing in 1975, when he reached his cynical agreement with the Shah which abandoned the Iraqi border claims but preserved Iraqi control of Kurdistan. Saddam was later to recall a conversation with Idris Barzani, son of the old Kurdish Democratic Party leader, in which he had warned of what would happen: 'If we fight, we shall win,' Saddam told Idris. 'Do you know why? ... You depended on our disagreement with the Shah of Iran. The root of the Iranian conflict is their claim to half of the Shatt al-Arab. If we could keep the whole of Iraq with the Shatt al-Arab, we would make no concessions. But, if forced to choose between half of the Shatt al-Arab and the whole of Iraq, then we will give away the Shatt al-Arab, in order to keep the whole of Iraq in the shape we wish it to be.' It was an argument which was equally applicable in 1990.

All Iraq's eastern and northern neighbours – Iran, Syria and Turkey – saw the crisis as a means of improving their own international situation. Iran was in the best position of all, courted by Iraq and by the West, able to do much as it liked because of the political in-fighting going on in Tehran which allowed the government to blame opposition groups if anything was done which offended the UN resolutions or American preferences.

Turkey decided early on that it would throw in its lot with the West, and did not make any overtures to Baghdad. Turkish policy during the crisis was as opaque as that of Iraq, and for the same reason: it was made and implemented by one man, the president, Turgut Ozal. Regarded as one of the most brilliant economists of his generation in Europe, Ozal was the man who, as prime minister, took Turkey back to democracy when the generals returned to their barracks in 1983, after having taken power three years earlier to avert civil war. Totally sure of his own abilities and scornful of the efforts of others, Ozal manoeuvred himself into the presidency on the retirement of General Kenan Evren, the former chief of staff, and continued to run the country as a one-man show.

Iraq's invasion of Kuwait at first seemed a disaster for Ozal and for Turkey. During the eight years of the Gulf war Turkey had walked a careful tightrope, maintaining relations with Iraq and Iran, trading with both, and extracting all the advantage it could from the Gulf crisis. During that time, Iraq doubled the capacity of the oil pipeline carrying crude from Kirkuk to the Mediterranean across Turkey, thus substantially increasing the royalties due to Ankara as well as ensuring a steady supply of relatively cheap oil. At the same time, Turkish construction companies became increasingly involved in projects in Iraq, transport firms set up regular services to Iraq and on to Kuwait, and Turkish farmers and manufacturers found better markets for their goods in Iraq than in Iran, which was still in difficulties two years after the end of the Gulf war.

By 1990, Turkey was selling goods worth $100 million to Kuwait, while its exports to Iraq were worth $750 million. Even Washington, anxious to minimize the effect of the embargo against Iraq upon its allies, agreed that sanctions would cost Turkey some $2 to $3 billion a year. The effect could be seen plainly in the southern port of Mersin, which used to handle between 60,000 and 100,000 tonnes of cargo a month for Iraq; once sanctions were applied, there was a total ban on all shipments. Again, some 5,000 lorries used to cross the border between Turkey and Iraq each day; within ten days, that figure was down to one or two. The reason, as with so many things in Turkey, was an Ozal decision: a total application of sanctions, instead of the sort of compromise favoured by King Hussein in Jordan, which involved the UN escape clause allowing humanitarian goods to continue to be traded.

Ozal believed he had found the way ahead for his country: he thought he could use the crisis to rescue Turkey from its increasing economic difficulties, and at the same time achieve major foreign policy objectives. The chief of these was to end once and for all the insurgency in eastern Turkey, where for two years the PKK, the Kurdish Workers Party, had been carrying on a revolt which by mid-1990 had reached the proportions of an uprising, a Turkish intifada. Based in Syria, the fighters of Abdullah Ocalan's PKK had the support of the local people, and safe bases across the borders in Iraq as well as Syria. Ozal believed that with Turkey and Syria on the same side, that haven might soon be denied to the Kurds, and that, furthermore, the defeat of Iraq would enable Turkey to take control of the northern areas of that country which are populated by the Kurds, if not directly then certainly through its influence on a reconstituted government in Baghdad.

There would also be economic advantages, Ozal believed, basing much of his optimism on assurances given by James Baker, who visited Ankara a week after the crisis began. Keeping his cards very close to his chest as usual, Ozal had long meetings in private with Baker; exactly what was said at those sessions intrigued the Turks, and worried many of them. What emerged in public was that Turkey would get cash from the United States for arms, soft loans and support for its application to join the European Community. Baker also promised to support the release to Turkey of a World Bank credit of $1.4 million held up because Turkey had not met the bank's economic criteria, and he said the United States would now go ahead with delivery of forty Phantom fighter-bombers held up since 1984 because of objections from Greece.

There were, it seemed, other promises made or understandings reached, but no one ever knew what they were, and eventually two members of the Turkish cabinet, defence minister Safa Giray and foreign minister Ali Bozer, resigned in protest at Ozal's refusal to tell them what was going on, or to allow them to take part in negotiations.

One indication of what might have been discussed came when Ozal presented to parliament a bill allowing the president to invite foreign troops into Turkey or to deploy Turkish forces abroad. It was, said Ozal, merely a precautionary move. The same excuse was given by the chief of staff, General Necip Torumtay, when it was noted that tanks had been moved to the Iraqi border and new missile defences installed around the NATO bases in southern Turkey, used mainly by the Americans. 'We are only taking precautions against the worst-case scenario,' the general said.

President Ozal believed he had such firm assurances from the Americans that the hardships being suffered by Turkey would all be worthwhile. He did not say what the rewards would be, leaving people to speculate. The most popular theory was that Ozal had won American backing for Turkey's claims in the Aegean, and that if, at some time in the future, Turkey were to threaten to use force, there would be no help for the Greeks from Washington.

In Syria, President Assad seized the moment to change overnight the fortunes of his desperately poor country. With his army bogged down in Lebanon, virtually abandoned by the Soviet Union, and with the economy in near-terminal condition, Syria was in no position to achieve the central objective of President Assad's long-term strategy – to regain the Golan Heights, which had been seized by Israel in 1967. A close ally of Iran during the Gulf war, mainly because of his opposition to Iraq, Assad had begun to improve his relations with Egypt and Jordan, and so, he hoped, with the West. Now he lost no time in lining up with the moderate Arab states: he voted at the Arab League and in the UN for action against Iraq, and sent 15,000 Syrian troops to Saudi Arabia as part of the Arab contingent. His immediate reward was a visit from James Baker, though many pointed out that Syria was still on the list of those countries deemed by America to sponsor state terrorism. That made no difference to the cordial talks between the two men, at which Assad made plain his hope that once the Gulf crisis was over, other problems would be resolved . . . The Golan was uppermost in his mind.

Israel remained diplomatically quiet as the crisis unfolded: the Americans realized that Israeli involvement would jeopardize the Arab consensus they were building, and would make it impossible for Arab countries to send troops to Saudi Arabia. Yet the Israelis did draw a line which would give Saddam Hussein a final opportunity if in desperation he sought to involve them: they announced that if any Iraqi troops moved into Jordan, then that would be a casus belli. It was something the Iraqis bore in mind, still hoping that opposition to Israel could unite the Arabs. Iraqi propaganda constantly harped on the links between America and Zionism, and talked of the conspiracy between Israel and America to carve up the Arab nation. Certainly Israel had an interest in seeing Iraq controlled.

During the early days of the Gulf war Israel had actively helped Iran, hoping that two of its most powerful opponents would exhaust each other. Yet both had emerged from the long conflict with powerful armies intact, and as opposed to Israel as ever, though Iraq was both the strongest and the most belligerent. From the Israeli point of view it was Iraq which had to be contained; and the way to do that was to encourage America to take military action. The result was a good deal of disinformation and straightforward misinformation from Israel: intelligence estimates passed on to the West constantly inflated Iraqi strength and Iraqi capabilities, and sought to show that Iraq was bent on further expansion.

What worried Israel most of all was that Iraq might suddenly conform to the UN resolutions, that it might withdraw from Kuwait without any conditions. If that happened, the embargo would have to be lifted, and everything would be back to square one. Except that the situation would be worse for Israel. Iraq would be there with its armies intact, its chemical weapons factories still producing, and its scientists continuing their work in developing nuclear capability. Above all, Iraq and the other Arabs would all be pressing the UN to act over other resolutions as it had over Resolution 660 – in other words, to bring the full power of the international community to bear on Resolution 242, which calls on Israel to withdraw from the territories occupied in 1967.

Even if Iraq were to be defeated militarily, the possibility of UN action remained a nightmare for the rightwing government in Israel. Shamir and the Likud party had no intention of giving up the West Bank – many of them thought the space vital to resettle the hundreds of thousands of Soviet Jews who poured into the country following the easing of Soviet exit restrictions and the imposition of tight controls on immigration by America and other countries of first choice for the Jews leaving Russia. An Iraqi withdrawal from Kuwait without a fight was the worst-case scenario for the Israelis, but even a defeated and broken Iraq left its problems, for then the Arab countries which had helped America, led by Syria, would be pressing for their reward, which not only meant the return of the Golan in the case of Syria, but also the establishment of a Palestinian homeland in the West Bank and Gaza.

There were other gains and losses for Israel too. The intifada uprising in the West Bank which began in 1987, had begun to run out of steam, with the factions loyal to the PLO in the occupied territories losing ground to Hamas, the Islamic grouping which took a far harder line, and which worried the moderate Palestinians as much as it did the Israelis. The shabab, the stone-throwing boys who were the spearhead of the intifada, had demonstrated that Israel could not hope to subjugate a people for ever, and by enlisting the sympathies of the Arabs living in Israel proper, had threatened to spread disorder beyond the West Bank and Gaza. But the impact of the uprising had not been translated into political gains: the dialogue between the PLO and the Americans in Tunis had yielded nothing, and the indications were that a younger, tougher leadership would take over and turn to more drastic action. The Gulf crisis was welcome to Israel because it removed the spotlight from the West Bank and Gaza, and also because it seemed to be leading to the final demise of the old PLO leadership.

Arafat and his ageing group of advisors who had established Fatah in Kuwait thirty-five years earlier felt bound to give total support to Saddam Hussein. They did so partly because they were beholden to Iraq, and partly to reflect popular Palestinian opinion in the occupied territories. It was a short-sighted move, and one which showed considerable ingratitude to Kuwait, a country which had the largest Palestinian expatriate population after Jordan, which had devoted millions to the Palestinian cause, and which had over the years been a champion to the PLO in international meetings.

But the Palestinians saw in Saddam Hussein a new breed of Arab leader, a man who did what he said he would do, who stood up to the Americans and the Israelis, and who seemed to them to offer the best hope of forcing concessions out of the Israeli government. Even so, the PLO leadership could have moderated its voice. But Arafat decided he had to give unqualified support, perhaps afraid for his own position – or even his own safety – if he did not. That decision lost him the last chance he had of becoming the first president of an independent Palestine. Early on, America and Israel decided that no matter what happened, the old guard of the PLO would never again be a party to negotiations; the Americans, over Israeli objections, said that when the time came to begin talking about the question of Palestine – as it certainly would – then representatives would be found in the occupied territories, or among those whom the Israelis had expelled. Faced with a tougher American attitude than any that had been experienced for years, the Israelis were forced to agree, just as they had to recognize that when it was all over, Israel and Palestine would once again go to the top of the international agenda, and that this time they would be unable to spin things out, or to expect that some act of sabotage by extremists would halt the process.

Hosni Mubarak, the Egyptian leader, had a far easier row to hoe. The inclinations of his people matched exactly the policy to which he was committed, and which he believed would bring the greatest rewards for Egypt. As early as the 1970s Egyptian farmers had been moved to southern Iraq, where their experience of farming in the Nile Delta enabled them to show their Iraqi neighbours how to get the maximum returns from the wetlands north of Basra. Then during the Gulf war, Egyptians in their hundreds of thousands went to Iraq to replace men serving in the armed services, to supply the middle management in Iraq's emerging service industries, or to use their skills in Iraq's rapidly expanded arms factories – the Egyptian munitions factory at Helwan outside Cairo was the first in the Arab world.

Eventually, there were more than two million Egyptians in Iraq. And almost all of them had returned to their homeland with sad tales of the way they had been treated – and often, cheated – forced into the army, sent to Basra to repair the canals there while the city was under artillery bombardment, or in the end, attacked by Iraqis returning from the war who resented Egyptians in their old jobs. At one stage, the Iraqis stopped Egyptian workers sending remittances home because of the desperate state of the Iraqi economy; at another time, hundreds of Egyptians were killed by returning Iraqi soldiers, and the authorities tried to hide it from the Egyptian government. For all the support given by Hosni Mubarak to Saddam Hussein during the Gulf war, for all the profits made, there was no love lost between Egypt and Iraq by the time of the invasion of Kuwait.

Yet there was calculation as well as popular sentiment in President Mubarak's policy. The peace which his predecessor, Anwar Sadat, had made with Israel had brought no real political dividends, and very few economic rewards either. Mubarak had managed to return Egypt to the Arab fold, but he had not re-established his country's leadership, nor had he made the economic breakthrough needed. He believed a wholehearted policy of supporting the West would achieve both. By agreeing to send troops to fight with the Americans – the first Arab country to do so – Mubarak earned the gratitude of the world superpowers and a promise of increased aid in the future. And by setting an example which many followed, he again demonstrated Egyptian leadership in the Middle East. The immediate reward was an American promise to write off $7 billion which Egypt owed the United States for arms, while the Arab Gulf states forgave a similar debt of $6.7 billion.

Domestically, it did him no harm either: the fundamentalists in Egypt, the Muslim Brotherhood, were becoming increasingly troublesome, and the prospect of a war led to a revulsion of feeling against them, while sending his troops on active service did wonders for army morale, and occupied any generals who might have become impatient.

At the far corners of the Arab world, in Yemen and in the Maghreb, attitudes were again ambivalent – the further from the possibility of fighting, the greater the scope for debate. Yemen gave qualified support to Iraq because it feared the presence of American troops in the Arabian peninsula, and because it was the only Arab country to have fought with Iraq against Iran. In the Maghreb, Algeria was opposed in principle to outside interference in Arab affairs. King Hassan of Morocco, for all his friendship with Washington and his determination to send troops, had to look over his shoulder at his own dissident extremists, and probably also feared the consequences of a war in the Gulf and the American-imposed order which might follow it. He took seriously his position as chairman of the Jerusalem committee, whose task is to restore the holy city to Arab control. Libya sided with Iraq against the American build-up, though even the unpredictable and eccentric Colonel Gaddafi did condemn the Iraqi invasion and annexation of Kuwait.

One immediate casualty of all these divisions was the Arab League. Both the secretary general, Chadli Klebi, and the League's ambassador in Washington, Clovis Maksoud, resigned as an early result of the quarrels which broke out. Rival factions called meetings, moves to return the League's headquarters to Cairo were bitterly opposed by Iraq and its supporters, and every meeting was the scene of rows – one so bad that a minister had a heart attack. At the crucial Cairo meeting on 10 August at which the decision was taken to back the UN sanctions against Iraq, and to send troops to help America defend Saudi Arabia, the voting was twelve to eight, with the PLO, Jordan, Algeria, Tunisia, Yemen, Libya, Mauritania, and Sudan backing Iraq. That split was repeated on 30 August 1990, when there was a debate on moving the League's head-quarters from Tunis, where it was transferred in 1979, back to Cairo. With that final vote, and the acrimony which surrounded it, the Arab League ceased to exist as an effective forum, and became merely a cover for those Arab countries which thought alike about the situation in the Gulf to meet together as and when they wanted.

In the days immediately before the invasion, the Kuwaitis felt under pressure not only from Iraq but also Saudi Arabia. Soon after Saudi Arabia and Iraq had concluded their non-aggression treaty, the Saudis had brought up their own demand for part of Kuwaiti territory – the small island of Qaruh in the southern part of Kuwait, long claimed by the Saudis and once briefly occupied. Now threatened in the north by Iraq, and aware of the pact between the Saudis and Saddam, the Kuwaitis were suddenly faced with an ultimatum from Riyadh for settlement of the undefined maritime border between the two countries, important because of the possibility of more off-shore oil finds. It was all the worse because it came at a time of deteriorating relations between Kuwait and Saudi Arabia, which had executed a number of Kuwaitis despite pleas for clemency. For Saddam, on the other hand, the sudden resurrection by Saudi Arabia of its demands on Kuwait – certainly an opportunistic move as Iraq put on the pressure through its mobilization at the time of the OPEC meeting – was just one more signal that there would be little trouble if he acted.

The Crisis of Gulf Security

The Kuwait crisis demonstrated the limitations of the political expediency which had governed international relations in the Cold War era. In the conflict between East and West, the countries of the Third World were regarded as pawns in a game of superpower chess, exploited by one or other power, no matter what suffering was imposed on their people. As Truman said of the Nicaraguan dictator, Anastasio Somoza, he might be a son of a bitch, but he was America's son of a bitch.

So it was in the Middle East. Every political convulsion in that region was seen as a plus or a minus in the great geo-political game, depending on whether it was viewed from Moscow or from Washington. The advantage ebbed and flowed; 'Soviet-backed' Egypt under Nasser became 'US-backed' Egypt under Sadat; Iraq was lured into the Soviet camp in the early 1970s, only to emerge as a Western 'asset' in the struggle to contain Iran. Symbiotic relationships developed between superpower patrons and dicta-torial client regimes which took little or no account of local realities or aspirations.

It was a situation in which the West was prepared to back undemocratic, right wing regimes on the basis of their anti-Communism, while the Soviet bloc was ready to support any dictator prepared to pay lip-service to a spurious 'anti-imperialism' in return for Kremlin backing. It meant that regimes of either hue could gain advantage by playing off one superpower against the other; a well-timed visit to Moscow by a leader ostensibly in the Western camp would often have the effect of eliciting better treatment by Washington. The golden rule, of course, was never to challenge both superpowers at once.

Many of these superpower–client relationships began to unravel as the Cold War came to a close. This was most obvious in eastern Europe, where entrenched Communist regimes fell one after the other in the face of popular protest once Moscow withdrew its support. The hope in the rapidly enlarging free world was that dictators everywhere would be forced to change if they were to survive. Some regimes did adapt, moving away from the rigid concepts of one-party or one-man rule in response to growing internal dissent inspired, at least in part, by the events in eastern Europe.

In the Arab world, elections were held in Algeria and Jordan, but the main beneficiaries in both countries were Islamic fundamentalists. This was in part a reflection of the Islamic revival in an Arab world grown tired of the slogans of secular pan-Arabists. But it also showed that in societies where conventional party politics were stifled, only the mosque could survive as a breeding ground for political dissent.

Iraq too began to pay lip service to the democratizing trend; almost as soon as the war with Iran was over Saddam announced, in November 1988, that the Baath Party had approved the doctrine of political pluralism which would lead to a multi-party state. Elections were held the following April for a legislative assembly which would ratify a new constitution providing freedom of assembly and expression. At the time Saddam may have felt confident enough to consider a degree of relaxation, though his moves were widely regarded as mere window-dressing. In reality the regime remained as totalitarian as ever and promises of greater democracy sat uneasily with the announcement, shortly before the Kuwait invasion, that Saddam was to be made president for life.

Saddam Hussein recognized earlier than most in the Arab world the dangers inherent in a changing world order. But even he must have been shocked by the speed with which the Communist regimes of eastern Europe collapsed in 1989, and the inability of secret police forces such as the Stasi in East Germany and

Securitate in Romania – both of which had helped set up the machinery of oppression in Iraq – to stop the rot.

Concern in the Arab world about the break-up of the Soviet empire had become almost an obsession. Even nominally pro-Western states were alarmed at the loss of the Soviet counterweight in regional affairs. In the past, the threat of superpower conflict caused by a regional war in the Middle East had occasionally obliged the Americans to impose some restraint on Israel. Now it seemed that the Soviet Union as well as the United States was actively supporting Israel, at least to the extent of allowing its Jews to emigrate there.

Saddam himself feared that the end of the Cold War would allow the United States to dictate terms in the Gulf and to thwart his own ambition to become the regional superpower.

In a speech in November 1989 he said that a representative of 'a big power' had come to Iraq to question its need for a large army.

> Our answer to this is that we want this big army so that no one can come and tweak our moustaches or pull our beards, and so that we can cut off the hand that tries to do this. This is all we want; we do not want to attack anybody, and we do not have ambitions outside Iraq. This army is for defending Iraq and the Arab whose moustache is tweaked and the Arab who wants us to support him and whom we believe has a rightful claim to that support.

It was a theme which Saddam continued to develop in subsequent months, through the Arab summit in Baghdad and right up to the invasion of Kuwait: Iraq under Saddam's leadership was taking upon itself the role of pan-Arab protector and enforcer in an increasingly perilous world.

'The theory of the superpowers says the stronger we are, the more capable we are of ensuring peace,' said Saddam. 'If they want to remove this theory from the world, we will remove it as well.'

The message he gave his fellow Arab leaders was that he was under attack by a superpower–Zionist conspiracy bent on preventing the emergence of Arab power. The conspirators had picked on him because he was already the strongest, and therefore the Arabs were obliged to back him.

This sham doctrine was exposed by Saddam's invasion of Kuwait, a gamble which he felt obliged to take out of economic necessity, but one which might have done better had he delayed for several years until he had become militarily stronger in relation to outside powers. In 1990, the so-called 'peace dividend' – the benefit envisaged from reducing armed forces as a result of the end of the Cold War – had not been cashed; the United States and the European powers still had large standing armies equipped with the world's most sophisticated weaponry, and the relaxation of tension in Europe allowed them rapidly to switch forces to the new theatre of operations in the Gulf.

If Saddam had waited long enough, the United States might have retreated into a new isolation in which it would cease to act as a world power. The question of the future role of the United States was a familiar theme of commentaries in the first half of 1990. American power and influence were rapidly being eclipsed by events elsewhere in the world: Japan was not only an established economic power, it seemed to be buying up much of the US economy; Europe was enlarged and strengthened by the unification of Germany and the emergence of democratic regimes in the East; soon the west Europeans could look forward to bidding farewell to the US forces which had served as the continent's first line of defence for forty-five years.

Then came the invasion of Kuwait, and in August 1990, none but the United States could have provided the leadership and the manpower for the international response that followed. Even so, President Bush might have faltered, given the magnitude of the enterprise. As it was, he was criticized for not allowing enough time for the Arabs to find a resolution of the crisis, although it was difficult to see how they could have found any diplomatic solution acceptable to Saddam except one that gave him what he wanted.

The speed and vigour of Bush's response nevertheless begged the question of its motivation; was his intention to lead the international community in righting a patent wrong? Or was he merely interested in restoring a regime in Kuwait which served US interests? Was there a real threat to the security of Saudi Arabia? If so, was not the United States preparing the ground for an oil war in which it could take control over all the oil resources of the Middle East?

The Americans did have a real fear of one state controlling such a vast share of the world's remaining oil resources, all the more important as supplies begin to run out in north and central America and in the North Sea. The impact of the Gulf war had already forced many Western countries into energy-saving policies. The crisis occurred in a time of near recession, when strategic stocks had been built up to the maximum because of the Gulf war, and Mexican and North Sea wells were still pumping at full capacity; even so, the sensitivity of the oil market was such that there was an overnight rise in the oil price from $22 to $30 when Kuwait was invaded. The market only settled when Saudi Arabia and other producers pledged to make up the 4.3 million barrel a day shortfall caused by the embargo on Iraqi and Kuwaiti crude. It was another jolt to the planners of East and West, who realized that because dependence on Gulf oil was bound to increase, the stability of that region was a vital interest not just of America or of the Soviet Union, but of the world.

That was the perception of politicians increasingly learning to live and work together. The military did not always think the same way, and both in the Pentagon and the Soviet high command there were still those who dreamed of taking control of Middle East oil, of securing the supply lines, or of ensuring the stability of the countries in which the oil was found.

Those who argued that the crisis was only about oil were usually people who had opposed the military response in the first place, though there was also a rare agreement between conservationists who argued that the crisis was a punishment for the West's profligate use of oil, and right wing isolationists, who claimed that environmental concerns had hampered US domestic production of oil and made the United States over-dependent on supplies from the Gulf.

But while the Western members of the anti-Iraq coalition were concerned about the future security of Gulf oil, there was also legitimate concern about the nature of the new world order which was now replacing the previous superpower rivalry. Arab and Third World states, even those involved in the coalition, were determined that the crisis should not give the Americans an opportunity to impose their hegemony on the Middle East. To counter this perception Bush tried to make the coalition as broad as possible, finally enlisting no less than twenty-six other countries in the expeditionary force.

As soon as the decision to commit American troops had been taken, at a two-hour meeting at Camp David on 4 August, Bush launched into a hectic round of personal diplomacy to win those allies. Most important of all, Bush then secured an agreement in principle from King Fahd to receive US forces in Saudi Arabia, although it was a week after the invasion before the king announced his decision to invite foreign troops to defend the kingdom.

Reading from a script on his desk and using none of the tricks of oratory that teleprompters permit, he said: 'The forces from friendly powers are here temporarily. They are here to help defend the kingdom and to participate in joint exercises, and they will leave here as soon as the kingdom so demands.'

It was a limp performance in a country little used to great matters of state being announced in television addresses. Usually, in Saudi Arabia, policies were allowed to evolve slowly, with soundings among different groups, and only brief and vague announcements cloaking rather than revealing in detail what had finally been decided. Now the king had no alternative: in the eastern provinces of the country people could see the planes flying in each day, and the American troops hurriedly digging in around the small town of Khafji, seven miles from the Kuwait frontier. In Jeddah and Riyadh, too, the traffic of diplomats and military officers from a dozen countries was plain for all to see; the king was merely putting into words what they all knew – not least because in Saudi Arabia, as in many other countries where the media is closely controlled, most people got their news from foreign radio stations.

Even now, the king found it difficult to say plainly that he had been forced to turn to the unbelievers, the Christians, to defend the holy places of Islam: 'The kingdom of Saudi Arabia expressed its desire for the participation of sister Arab forces and other friends,' was the circumlocution used. King Fahd did emphasize that the build-up was purely defensive: 'The dispatch of foreign troops to Saudi Arabia is directed against no one but is purely for defensive purposes prompted by the current situation facing the kingdom. We are determined to protect our territory and to safeguard our economic potential. We have to improve our defences.'

Then came a denunciation of Iraq's seizure of Kuwait, and a demand that Saddam Hussein should pull out and the legitimate government of the emirate be restored. 'The invasion of Kuwait was the most horrible aggression the Arab nation has known in its modern history. Iraq rendered homeless the people of Kuwait and afflicted them with insufferable pains.'

It was not a great speech by any means, but it did show that the king understood both what had to be done, and the consequences likely to flow from his decision. He was admitting that Saudi Arabia, which had become the biggest importer of arms in the world, could not defend itself, that all those sisterly Arab nations which had been supported by Saudi largesse were equally incapable of coming to the rescue, and that only America and its allies had either the means or the will to halt the Iraqis. The king ignored Saddam Hussein's assurances that he had no intention of moving on into Saudi Arabia, or the Iraqi leader's careful distinction between Iraq's historic claim to Kuwait and its friendly relations with the kingdom.

It was a bitter pill for the king and for all his people. For decades they had been used to buying themselves out of trouble, of being listened to respectfully and deferred to because of their wealth; suddenly they found money had no meaning, and might was all. The United States, the supporter of Israel, the state which prevented the third holiest shrine of Islam from returning to Muslim control, would now be responsible for the security of the holiest places,

Mecca and Medina. Jews in the American forces would have to be welcomed, brazen women soldiers tolerated, and unclean food, such as pork, allowed into the country.

In the Saudi way, religious leaders were soon found to justify the changed situation, and remove any blame which might attach to the king and the princes as Iraqi propaganda spoke day after day of the defiling of the Islamic shrines. The first religious seminar on the Gulf crisis was organized in Islamabad – Saudi money could still get some things done. Hundreds of Islamic scholars debated the issue, and then issued a fatwa approving the American presence in Saudi Arabia, denounced by fundamentalist groups as a desecration. 'The presence of the Americans is not against Islam,' said Wasi Mazhar Nadvi, a noted scholar and former religious endowments minister in Pakistan. 'Had the Americans not stopped the Iraqis, they would have captured the entire Saudi kingdom,' And the Iraqis, it was noted, were a secular people.

Similar meetings were held in Cairo and other capitals sympathetic to the kingdom, more fatwas and opinions were given, and the Saudi rulers could once again hold their heads high – safely behind America's Desert Shield.

As soon as King Fahd agreed to the American deployment, the 82nd Airborne was dispatched. This spearhead unit from Fort Bragg, North Carolina, was always the first to be sent in a sudden military crisis, but had been particularly trained in desert warfare in the Mojave when it was the core unit of the rapid deployment force, which had as its first task the defence of the Gulf oilfields. The swift arrival of the 82nd Airborne was intended to forestall any Iraqi takeover of the airfields in the eastern province of Saudi Arabia, or a quick drive on to Dhahran.

Yet there never seemed any danger of that. For all the talk of Saddam's plans to attack the kingdom, it never seemed likely. The Iraqi deployment, once Kuwait was taken, was entirely defensive, and the much-cited move towards the Saudi border was merely the pushing out of frontlines and tripwires which any prudent commander would undertake when setting up a defensive line. All the evidence was that suggestions of possible moves into Saudi Arabia by the Iraqis were merely propaganda designed to support the huge build-up of forces by America and its allies, which despite the talk of its defensive nature, was also aimed at the overthrow of Saddam Hussein and the destruction of Iraq's military potential. The much-vaunted idea that the allied forces were deployed for defence alone could hardly be sustained if there was no evidence of any danger of attack; and over the months, the Iraqis, both the leaders in Baghdad and the commanders in Kuwait, went out of their way to avoid any incident which might have given a casus belli. Equally, if the Iraqis had wanted to move into the kingdom, they could easily have seized the airfields at the same time as their invasion of Kuwait; they had the airborne forces available which would have been capable of taking landing fields and holding them the few hours until they could be reinforced overland, making it impossible for the Saudi forces to counter-attack successfully. There was no evidence that this was ever their intention.

Deployment of the 82nd Airborne was both rapid and easy, and with the airfields and ports secure, the build-up began. Air cover was ensured by carrier-based planes, and intelligence was provided by KH11 and KH12 satellites, the AWACS reconnaissance planes based in Saudi Arabia, and the Hawkeye and Orion aircraft flying out of Diego Garcia. After some initial confusion the diplomats managed to persuade enough Arab countries to contribute troops to give the allied force in the kingdom a respectable mix – Egypt, Syria and Morocco all sent units to join the 60,000 strong Saudi army, while France and Britain led the European response. The actual movement of men and equipment was less efficient than the American public relations men made out: commercial aircraft had to be chartered to get all the units in position quickly enough, while America alone could not provide all the merchant shipping tonnage needed to transport the armoured divisions either from continental America or from Germany. In the end, Greece provided the largest number of ships.

A congressional report was highly critical of the military sealift command, which is responsible for supplying ammunition as well as moving armour and vehicles. So frequent were the breakdowns of ships, so inefficient the labour force in loading them, that the target date of 15 October when the US forces were supposed to be ready for anything, including a sustainable attack on Iraq, was pushed back by about three weeks. According to a congressional study, the United States was very lucky that it did not face 'an attack situation' and so had time to get things on the ground.

Rear-Admiral Eugene Carroll rather gave the game away in his evidence to Congress when he described the build-up in Saudi Arabia as 'the creation of an offensive war-fighting force directed at Iraq'. A truly defensive and truly international effort would not have required such a massive sea-lift, he said. Certainly the effort was a huge one: some 800,000 tonnes of material had to be moved in the initial phase, followed by 1.7 million tonnes for a sustained presence.

Other difficulties surfaced as more forces moved into the Arabian peninsula. Most stemmed from the fact that since the end of the Second World War in 1945, United States planning had been based on the idea of fighting in Europe. There, huge numbers of troops and vast supplies of equipment could be stored ready for any emergency, so that the shortcomings of the air- and sea-lift capacities encountered in Operation Desert Shield would not have mattered. Other problems were due to the equipment being used. Designed primarily as static defences to stop an attack by Warsaw Pact forces from eastern Europe in a developed environment, possibly in winter, the army's heavy tanks and guns were not ideal for the kind of offensive operations which might have to be launched. There was little special equipment for desert conditions, so helicopters had to have make-shift filters fitted to avoid sand, and even then to be given quick services every couple of hours; computers often had to be wrapped in cold cloths to maintain performance, and specially adapted and air-conditioned hangars had to be erected for immediate-readiness strike aircraft.

The most important American weapon, and one deployed early and successfully, was the A10 tank-buster, known as 'the Brute' to those who fly it. It is almost a flying tank itself, armoured to absorb damage that would knock any other plane out of the sky.

Developed as a counter to Soviet tank superiority in Europe, the A10 has a 30mm cannon which can fire 3,000 shells a minute, and carries a huge weight of anti-tank weapons, though they had not been tested against the Soviet T72 tanks operated by the Iraqis. The T72s, heavier than the American Abrams, had their own problems of overheating in desert conditions, and were used mainly as dug-in, hull-down defence positions during the Gulf war.

As Washington sent its diplomats around its allies to preach the virtues of burden-sharing, one quiet windfall from the Gulf crisis was being noted by American Congressmen from states with factories producing armaments. Suddenly, with the dollar low in the international markets and oil revenues soaring, new arms orders began to come in as governments responded to the crisis by beefing up their defences – Israel was not alone in cancelling a projected $20 million cut in arms expenditure. Israel also gave an indirect boost to the American arms industry: noting the scale of intended purchases by Saudi Arabia from America, the Israeli chief of staff, General Dan Shomron, said the Americans must balance all the new equipment being supplied to the Arabs by similar sales to Israel.

The loser in the arms stakes was Britain. Without fanfare, the Saudis announced that they were signing a $20 billion deal with the United States, which included the purchase of another 385 Abrams tanks to add to the 315 already on order. They also let it be known that in future they would abandon their policy of diversified arms procurement, which looked to France and Britain as well as America, and would from then on rely on their chief ally. To show they meant what they said, they warned that the final tranche of the Al-Yamama contract with Britain for forty-eight Tornadoes would probably not go ahead, a loss to Britain of some $3 billion. The cancellation broke no contracts, as the final stage was only initialled in a memorandum of understanding, but it was an ignominious end to the 'arms deal of the century', and was a particularly bitter blow, coming just as Britain announced the dispatch of the 7th Armoured Brigade, the Desert Rats, from Germany to the Gulf.

Growing Third World and Arab fears that the American build-up was part of a neo-colonialist enterprise were fed by propaganda from Baghdad, with the Iraqi regime casting itself in the heroic role of defender of the poor against greedy Western powers and tight-fisted and reactionary Arabs. These fears were scarcely calmed by some incautious statements from the Bush administration concerning Washington's ideas on maintaining the peace after the crisis was over. While many hailed the 'rebirth' of the United Nations as an effective instrument for ensuring international order, there was a distinct tendency in the US administration to see America's role as the policeman of that order, with the added refinement that, in future, the rest of the world would have to pick up the bill.

On 4 September, James Baker addressed the House of Representatives Foreign Affairs Committee about future security arrangements in the Gulf, and perhaps in an effort to calm the worries expressed, spoke of the need to strengthen the ability of Gulf nations to resist future aggression on their own, so that American soldiers did not have to remain indefinitely in the desert. The speech was read by some in the Middle East as the announcement of an American-imposed settlement of the region's problems which would primarily be designed to guarantee US interests.

That was how it was seen in Iran, where it prompted Ayatollah Ali Khamanei, the spiritual leader, to denounce what he described as American attempts to dominate the Gulf. Describing the struggle against the American presence as a jihad or holy war, he said: 'The United States has been busy digging in the Persian Gulf for a long time and this is not acceptable to us or to any other nation in the region. Muslim people will never allow the United States to create defensive and security systems in the region and will fight American greed and domination of the Persian Gulf.'

Khamenei's statement was couched in the customary intemperate tones of the Iranian revolutionary leadership and it immediately sent a frisson through the coalition amid fears that it presaged the creation of an Iran–Iraq axis – a fairly unlikely result given the antipathy between the two. In fact, Khamenei had been making what was, from the Iranian perspective, a perfectly reasonable point – ousting Iraq from Kuwait was one thing but indefinite US domination of the Gulf was another. 'What right do they have to say they must safeguard the security of the region, and that the continued security of the region requires them to be here?' said Khamenei. 'What business is it of theirs?' After that Washington seemed to temper its enthusiasm for promoting long-term solutions.

When Baker addressed the House committee his mind had been on America's partnership with the Soviet Union in tackling the crisis, as the date for a Bush–Gorbachev summit approached. 'I do not know where we would be if it were not for the co-operation and enlightened new thinking of the Soviet leadership,' he said.

The terms of that relationship were discussed at Helsinki in early September at a summit called to define the new world order, though Bush's immediate motive was to make it clear to Saddam that he could not hope to gain by playing off the Soviet Union against the United States. Gorbachev agreed, but the continued influence of foreign policy hardliners, particularly in the Soviet military, made it impossible for him to give open approval for US action in the Gulf.

The two sides were agreed on the need to reverse the invasion but the Soviets were less sure about the desirability of toppling Saddam, which appeared to be part of the US programme. What emerged from Helsinki was a dual approach in which the United States took the tough, intransigent line towards Saddam while Moscow continued to try to persuade him that only by withdrawing from Kuwait could he hope to derive any benefit from the crisis. It sometimes seemed that the Soviets were going soft on Iraq but, in fact, they did not waver from the demand for a total withdrawal from Kuwait.

On his return from Helsinki, Bush told Congress confidently: 'Iraq will not be permitted to annex Kuwait. That's not a threat, or a boast, that's just the way it's going to be.'

Yet Moscow was angered when Margaret Thatcher suggested that sanctions might have to remain in place after a withdrawal in view of Saddam's possession of chemical and biological weapons and his nuclear aspirations. The Soviets complained – although not publicly – that this left Saddam no way out should he eventually decide to sue for peace.

Mikhail Gorbachev's main concern as the crisis developed was to strengthen his relationship with the United States as an antidote to his increasing domestic problems. Washington, for its part, was committed to helping Gorbachev to survive, not least as a preferable alternative to the uncertainties of a disintegrating Soviet Union. Moscow also had to bear in mind its own geo-political interests in the Gulf, which lies on its southern flank. Following the Iranian revolution and the Gulf war, it was clear that the political turmoil that would stem from a war, or from the overthrow of Saddam, would pose a further threat to the already unstable southern Soviet republics. Moscow had spent a decade cultivating the friendship of the conservative Gulf states and had no wish – even in the light of the new superpower relationship – to see the Gulf become an American lake. Moscow therefore had an interest in the survival of Saddam's regime, though in a weakened form. The Americans, on the other hand, wanted his downfall, but had only vague notions of what should replace him.

The weak opposition to Saddam within Iraq did not seem to present a viable alternative. Most were in exile, where they had failed in the past to achieve any common programme against Saddam. In response to the crisis they met for almost three weeks in Damascus during October, to try to work out a common position. The groups represented were from the Islamic, Kurdish and leftist movements among the one million Iraqi Arabs and 250,000 Kurds who had fled Saddam's Iraq. The Islamic movements included the supreme council of the Islamic Revolution led by Mohammed Bakr Hakim based in Tehran, the Islamic Action Organization and Daawa. For the Kurds, there was the Patriotic Union of Kurdistan led by Jalal Talabani, and the Kurdish Democratic Party of Masoud Barzani plus four other smaller groups united in the Kurdish National Front. On the left was the Iraqi Communist party led by Aziz Mohammed, while nationalist interests were represented by the Syrian regional command of the Baath Party. In the end, there was very little agreement, though according to Hosha Zebari, the

KDP's European spokesman, the group did agree on 'the need to oust Saddam and install parliamentary rule after an interim administration lays the groundwork for free elections'.

Beyond that, delegates could not even agree at first on the size and membership of a proposed executive committee. They were divided on sanctions and whether force should be used against Iraq, and unclear on how to proceed after Saddam was toppled. 'We are against sanctions that hurt ordinary Iraqis', said the Shia human rights activist Abdul Shibab al-Hakim. 'They are not responsible for Saddam's atrocities. We don't want Western military intervention because Iraqis along with Westerners and Arabs will be killed.'

The Communists objected to the demand by Daawa that the phrase 'In the name of God, the Compassionate, the Merciful', be incorporated as a slogan of the united opposition. Elsewhere, Western-style democratic parties, such as the New Umma Party, led by Saad Jabr, the son of a pre-revolution prime minister, refused to contemplate an alliance with the Communists and the anti-Saddam Baathists.

The Damascus talks did finally settle on the creation of a seventeen-member council, to include eight Islamic representatives and nine secularists, of whom five were to be Kurds. But the absence of a defined programme was inauspicious. The opposition hoped to recreate the situation that existed before the 1958 revolution when a national front of opposition parties had been one of the catalysts for the overthrow of the monarchy. But in 1990, perhaps because of memories of past conflicts, it was an uphill struggle towards unity.

Although Daawa and the Communists claimed to have some organization still intact in Iraq, the years of repression had taken their toll. Daawa had nearly succeeded in assassinating Saddam in early 1989 when, together with his guests King Hussein and President Mubarak, he went to open a reconstruction project at Fao. A truckload of explosives, which would have killed all three men and probably many others besides, was discovered before it could be detonated. When we asked Abu Ali, Daawa's European representative, if the party had now abandoned the idea of assassination, he replied: 'We have the men and the intense desire to kill him. What we lack is the right arms and the right intelligence.'

At the time of the invasion of Kuwait, the only opposition group which could be said to have active guerrilla forces inside the country, albeit sorely depleted, was the Kurds. But the Kurdish leadership was wary of allying itself with the coalition opposing Saddam in view of its bitter past experience of relying on outside powers to support its cause. And similarly, the recent history of the Kurds could only serve as a warning to the superpowers that any attempts to manipulate minority opposition groups were doomed to failure.

After they were unwillingly incorporated into the new Iraqi state in the mandate period, the Kurds received no official recognition of their separate status until the 1958 revolution when a new constitution guaranteed Kurdish national rights. The honeymoon with the Qassem regime was shortlived; in 1961, in response to a crackdown on Kurdish institutions and the bombardment of Kurdish villages and towns, the Kurdish Democratic Party launched a rebellion – the so-called War of Liberation – which was to last, on and off, until 1975, when Saddam signed the Algiers agreement with the Shah.

The Baath regime often argued that of the countries with Kurdish minorities – the others are Turkey, Iran, Syria and the Soviet Union – Iraq was the only one which recognized the Kurds' right to autonomy. In fact the underlying trend of Baathist policy was the Arabization of the Kurdish region and its total economic and cultural incorporation into the modern Arab state. When the Baathists returned to power in 1968, with Hassan al-Bakr as president, a new offensive was launched and Kurdish peasants were once more expelled from their lands. But this time, the war against the Kurds threatened to undermine the regime's policy of establishing better relations with the Soviet Union. The KDP had historically been allied with the Iraqi Communist Party, gave asylum to its persecuted members and thus enjoyed the direct backing of Moscow. Now the Kremlin wanted to bring Baathist Iraq into an 'anti-imperialist' alliance in order to extend its influence in the

Middle East, but not unless the suppression of the Kurds ceased. It therefore proposed to use its good offices to bring about a reconciliation between the Baath and the KDP, and nominated as its mediator Yevgeni Primakov, the former *Pravda* journalist who twenty years later in the wake of the Kuwait invasion was to act as diplomatic go-between for Mikhail Gorbachev and Saddam Hussein.

The Soviet mediation led to the agreement of 11 March 1970 between the KDP and the Baath Party under which the latter recognized the Kurdish nation and promised Kurdish participation in government. But the agreement was never satisfactorily implemented and the war resumed in 1973. In the meantime, Saddam had reached a deal with his former arch-enemies, the Communists, to bring them into government under the umbrella of a Progressive National Front. This rapprochement was a direct result of the Treaty of Friendship and Co-operation signed with Moscow in 1972. The Kremlin had succeeded in gaining its foothold in Iraq and the Kurds were forgotten.

From 1973 until the Algiers agreement of 1975, the Kurds became unwilling pawns in a conflict between Washington and Moscow and their client states, Iran and Iraq, in which the Kurds themselves were the ultimate victims. With their former protector, the Soviet Union, allied with the oppressor and supplying him with arms, the Kurds were forced to turn elsewhere for support, so the KDP leader, Mustafa Barzani, reluctantly entered into an alliance with the Shah, whose interest lay in making life difficult for his radical neighbours in Iraq. Barzani wisely refused to put his trust in the Shah unless he had adequate guarantees from the United States that Iran would not abandon him in the future. President Nixon, on the advice of Secretary of State Henry Kissinger, agreed to support the Shah–Barzani alliance, and the CIA was ordered to provide finance for the operation. The Americans and the Iranians had no interest in a Kurdish victory. Their aim was merely to weaken Iraq and limit its opportunities for spreading its radical message throughout the region. According to a 1974 memorandum from the CIA: 'Both Iran and the US hope to benefit from an unresolvable situation in which Iraq is intrinsically weakened by the Kurds' refusal to give up their semi-autonomy. Neither Iran nor the US would like to see the situation resolved one way or the other.'

The Shah and the CIA supplied the Kurds with just enough military backing to keep the insurgency going. Barzani managed to build an army of 50,000 men, and the KDP was able to set up an independent administration in liberated areas. Eventually, the pressure from the Kurds became so great that Saddam Hussein decided to sue for peace and approached Egypt and Algeria as potential mediators between himself and the Shah. Kissinger was, by this time, involved in negotiating a disengagement between Egyptian and Israeli forces in the Sinai following the 1973 Middle East War. The US interest now lay, not so much in isolating Iraq as in persuading it to temper its opposition to an Egyptian–Israeli deal which Syria was trying to scuttle. The price to be paid for Iraqi compliance was for the United States and Iran to abandon the Kurds.

In the months before the Kuwait invasion Saddam again made tentative approaches through third parties to the rebel Kurds as part of his strategy of neutralizing potential threats. The Kurds refused the Iraqi offers, but once the crisis began, they acknowledged that they were prepared to accept any concessions Saddam might be forced, out of weakness, to grant them. Within the anti-Iraqi coalition, intelligence agencies raised the possibility of arming the Kurds across the Turkish frontier in the hope of creating a fifth column on the northern front in the event of war. The proposal was quietly vetoed by Turkey, concerned to avoid any move that might strengthen its own rebellious Kurdish minority.

In the end, the machinations of both Washington and Moscow failed to bring stability to the region. The Kuwait crisis and the changed international circumstances in which it occurred gave the world community a slender opportunity to redress the balance by confronting all the issues which plagued the region. The problem was that each regional participant in the grand coalition wanted something different from the crisis.

Egypt and Syria expected rewards once the Gulf crisis was

settled, clearly believing that a general settlement in the Middle East would be at the top of the agenda when it was all over. For Egypt, that meant at least carrying out Anwar Sadat's aim, frustrated by the Israeli interpretation of the Camp David accords, of obtaining a homeland for the Palestinians. Syria shared that goal, but had a more imperative national need – restoration of the Golan Heights, occupied and annexed by Israel.

Israel itself obeyed American instructions to maintain a low profile until on 8 October the indiscipline of its police force resulted in the horrific killings at the Dome of the Rock in Jerusalem, and shifted world attention back to the Arab–Israeli issue. For Israel, the objective was not just to get rid of Saddam Hussein, but to destroy Iraq's military capability, and in particular, its rocket technology. It was a bonus that the PLO and the Palestinians in the occupied territories supported Baghdad, as that meant that the PLO could be eliminated as a negotiating partner in the discussions bound to follow a settlement in the Gulf. But Israel realized that even if a military threat against it was removed, some of the rewards due to those who helped the United States would have to be provided by Israeli concessions. Yet to Israel, the overriding reality was that a failure to restrain Saddam Hussein now would be likely to lead to a more serious crisis in the future – in the worst case, a nuclear war between Israel and Iraq.

This was the ultimate dilemma which the international community, and particularly America, faced in the summer of 1990: to fight or to appease, to put preservation of the nascent new world order above all else, or to allow domestic anti-war pressures to dictate policy.

Opinion in the West was clouded by differing perceptions of Saddam Hussein. It was clear that many who opposed the massive build-up in the Gulf found it difficult to accept that the leader of a relatively small Arab state could pose a real threat to world peace. But this ignored Saddam's stated aspirations, his abilities and his achievements in building his modern Arab state. Here was a man who had manipulated a small and unrepresentative political grouping, the Baath, into a mass movement which controlled every institution in the state according to his personal bidding. He had built a vast army, survived a costly war, and refused to abandon his long-term ambitions because of short-term setbacks. He had also created a highly educated technocratic elite, who understood the West and were able to scour the world for all the latest in high technology. Everything the West had, particularly in the military field, Iraq would acquire – whether it was the latest in computerized command centres or nuclear triggers, which might one day form part of a bomb. He was on the way to having a satellite in space and he already had rockets which could theoretically hit southern Europe. As Saddam said after his troops invaded Kuwait – the world could not claim it had not been warned.

As time went on, voices were raised in favour of compromise, and an American-led campaign to prepare people for the horrors of war by giving casualty estimates rebounded when it led to a revulsion against the use of force at all. The 'elder statesmen' who visited Baghdad in efforts to secure the release of hostages were powerful advocates of negotiations.

American congressmen, sensitive to the shifts in public opinion in their states reflected in their postbags, began to question the need for war. In Europe, President Bush's apparently contradictory signals were seen as vacillation; in the United States, they were accepted as signs that the President was weighing public opinion as well as international imperatives.

The difficulty was that any talks or negotiations with Saddam would be bound to involve some form of compromise, some face-saving formula which would allow him to take his forces out of Kuwait without being subjected to total defeat. Against that, President Bush in the first weeks of the crisis had stressed that Saddam must not gain by his seizure of Kuwait. So even Saddam's increasingly desperate attempts to link the Palestine question to his invasion of Kuwait could not be openly allowed. There were assurances that once it was all over the other problems of the Middle East would have to be addressed, but this was not enough for Saddam. He had to be able to show his people some prize for their hardships, or go down to defeat. No middle way seemed possible.

The first mistake of the crisis, to many observers, was that the allies had left Saddam no way out, no possibility of retreat with honour. Diplomats said the first rule was always to leave your opponent an escape route, otherwise every confrontation would develop into a conflict. This was an unconvincing argument, and those who harked back to the 1930s seemed to have history on their side, even if no two crises are quite the same. Against this it was argued that Saddam Hussein had not only committed a blatant act of aggression against a weak neighbour which had given no credible grounds for attack, but that his past conduct had shown he could not be trusted to keep promises, to rule fairly, or to conform to accepted international norms.

Saddam Hussein wanted not just to be the dominant regional power, the protector of the Gulf; he sought to become the leader of the Arabs, and from that position, to build a wider Islamic alliance which would become a new force in international politics.

Iraq is a country which faces two ways – east to Iran and the Gulf, and west to the Fertile Crescent of the eastern Mediterranean. Kuwait was seen as one stepping stone on Saddam's way to fulfilment of his ambition; another would certainly be an eventual confrontation with Israel, or else with Syria. Meanwhile the peace with Iran remained fragile, despite his concessions to Tehran. In the future, if he were left alone, he would try to control the oil market as he did in Geneva in 1990. And he would surely use force or the threat of force to keep the Saudis in line at some time in the future given their position as the swing oil producer capable of out-pumping any other state. If Saddam were not stopped after his rape of Kuwait, he would certainly have to be stopped later on.

All this was seen as plainly in Baghdad as in any other capital, and there were even those who in absolute privacy would admit that Iraq's claims to Kuwait might not stand up too well in an international court.

Yet there were other arguments too, mostly directed at the United States: why should America be able to impose its will when it clearly held a double standard? It had demonstrated, in the current crisis, that it was capable of effective diplomacy. It had secured the early backing of the United Nations, followed by swift and resolute action. But why was that ability so selectively applied? UN Resolution 242, calling for Israeli withdrawal from occupied Arab territory, was the example most usually given. By 1990 it had been on the books for twenty-three years, yet nothing had been done to enforce compliance; if oil were found in the West Bank or Gaza, might the situation change? The American answer was yes, of course; it would be idle to ignore realities. At the same time, past errors or inactivity should not be allowed to prevent action now.

Saddam launched his attack on Kuwait because he believed he could get away with it, and because he saw it as a path to future successes. Those who backed him – or at least, failed to condemn him – did so because they saw advantage for themselves, their countries, the region or 'the Arab cause'. None argued that what Saddam did was right. While many held that American actions were little better, the truth is that whatever the basic motives of the Americans might have been, they were acting legally, and they had the backing of the majority of the states of the world. If they had not acted, if they had left it all to the Arabs to sort out, there is little doubt that Saddam would have succeeded. Saddam may have emerged as a hero to radical Arab leaders, or to the Arab man in the souk, but that was only in comparison with his pale and inefficient contemporaries. He had begun as a bully-boy, and he remained one as head of state.

As the crisis evolved, there were ominous signs that the old question of how in future to ensure Gulf security was producing the same old answer – more weapons. At one level, the Western forces in the region were salesmen in a vast arms bazaar, encouraging local states to buy yet more modern weapons to guarantee their future security, even though the weapons they already possessed had singularly failed to deter Iraqi aggression in 1990. Iran, after all, had fought the Gulf war with weapons once supplied by America in order to ensure the security of the Gulf, and Iraq had of course used Western aircraft to sink Western shipping. And yet the arms build-up went on, with the eager participation of every arms-manufacturing country from both the Western and Eastern blocs.

It would be an unhappy irony if, in a new era of international co-operation, the world powers opted to return to the Cold War doctrine of ensuring peace in the Gulf through a precarious balance of hostile forces.

The real test will come over the next few years: if all the problems of the Middle East really are addressed in a spirit of dialogue rather than confrontation, if rational and practical solutions can be found which benefit all the people of the region, then there will be no more room for Saddam Hussein and his kind. If nothing is done, if the United States and its allies merely rely on arming potential belligerents and an occasional use of the big stick to keep order, then worse, no doubt, is yet to come.

After considerable American lobbying, on Thursday, 29 November 1990, the UN Security Council passed the following resolution by twelve votes to two against (Cuba and Yemen), with China abstaining:

> Recalling and reaffirming its Resolutions 660 (1990), 661 (1990), 662 (1990), 664 (1990), 665 (1990), 666 (1990), 667 (1990), 669 (1990), 670 (1990), 674 (1990), and 677 (1990),
>
> Noting that, despite all efforts by the United Nations, Iraq refuses to comply with its obligation to implement Resolution 660 (1990) and the above subsequent relevant Resolutions, in flagrant contempt of the Council,
>
> Mindful of its duties and responsibilities under the Charter of the United Nations for the maintenance and preservation of international peace and security,
>
> Determined to secure full compliance with its decisions, Acting under Chapter VII of the Charter of the United Nations,
>
> 1 Demands that Iraq comply fully with Resolution 660 (1990) and all subsequent relevant Resolutions and decides, while maintaining all its decisions, to allow Iraq one final opportunity, as a pause of good will, to do so;
>
> 2 Authorises member states co-operating with the Government of Kuwait, unless Iraq on or before 15 January, 1991 fully

implements, as set forth in Paragraph 1 above, the foregoing Resolutions, to use all necessary means to uphold and implement Security Council Resolution 660 (1990) and all subsequent relevant resolutions and to restore international peace and security in the area;

3 Requests all states to provide appropriate support for the actions undertaken in pursuance of Paragraph 2 of this Resolution;

4 Requests the states concerned to keep the Council regularly informed on the progress of actions undertaken pursuant to Paragraphs 2 and 3 of this Resolution;

5 Decides to remain seized of the matter.

Index